higher education: participants confronted

higher education: participants confronted

Josiah S. Dilley

University of Wisconsin
Madison

Wm. C. Brown Company Publishers

COUNSELING AND GUIDANCE SERIES

Consulting Editor

JOSEPH C. BENTLEY
The University of Utah

Copyright © 1970 by
Wm. C. Brown Company Publishers

ISBN 0–697–06125–6

Library of Congress Catalog Card Number: 79–114804

Printed in the United States of America

Contents

Preface

Screams of dissent and threats of violence have been hurled from college campuses by rebel students only to clash head-on with yells of rebuke and threats of retaliation from angry citizens. As the verbal, and sometimes physical, battle is watched with fascination by the "outside world," universities continue to function because professional participants in higher education continue to make daily decisions about hard-to-solve campus problems.

Thousands of words have been written about campus troubles, but relatively few words can be found which convey the complexity of the problems facing those who are directly involved. One can search the literature with little hope of finding guidelines which may help those who must make difficult decisions.

This book has been written for two reasons: (1) in the hope that it will partially fill the void that now exists around decision-making processes in higher education. People both in and out of the university need to become more aware of the problems which must be solved in modern university life; (2) as a resource for those seeking careers in higher education.

The book is a collection of thirty-six troublesome decision situations involving university presidents, deans, faculty members, student personnel workers, counselors, students, parents, and alumni. Although identifying characteristics have been altered to protect privacy, the cases tell the story of real people with real problems. They involve such issues as nudity, race relations, student power, drugs, faculty autonomy, confidentiality of information, grades, and violence. In each case the reader is asked to make his decision, then the actual solution is presented. Thus, the reader can compare his decision with that of the protagonist.

Acknowledgments

This book could not have been written without the help of colleagues and students of mine in various parts of the United States who, wittingly or unwittingly, supplied me with the raw material. I am most grateful for their help. I owe special thanks to Tom Hoover, Steve Saffian, Chan Young, Ranny Thrush, Dave Jepson, Dennis Tierney, Judy LeRoy, Jean Spangler, and Marilyn Dilley.

Introduction

Since October 1, 1964, when 500 Oakland police were called onto the Berkeley campus, universities have been under unprecedented attack. Students have initiated mass protests against "immoral and irrelevant" institutions. Citizens and legislators have had their own protests: handling of the student protest by university administrators; immorality on the campus; the continuing rise in costs of higher education. More recently, members of university faculties have criticized student protesters, legislators, and administrators who in turn are now criticizing the lack of understanding on the part of student groups, legislators, faculty groups, citizen groups, and so forth.

The longer the protester list grows, the more obvious it becomes that much of the protest and criticism is founded in a general misunderstanding of problems faced by participants in higher education today. One of the purposes of this book is to illuminate these problems and in addition, to facilitate a more understanding attitude toward those who are fighting. A basic assumption is that when people see positions and problems from the other's point of view, they are more likely to work harmoniously together toward making constructive changes.

Another purpose of the book is to provide training material for people contemplating careers in higher education. If they have had a chance to study critical issues and to simulate making decisions about controversial issues, then presumably they will become more competent participants. This book is not a philosophical treatise on the aches and pains of the modern university. It is a record of the personal confrontations with the wide gamut of complex and simple problems that must be solved daily by some member of every university community.

There are thirty-six troublesome decisions involving university presidents, deans, student personnel workers, faculty members, counselors, students and their parents, and alumni. The decisions are written as case

1

histories in the narrative style. The reader is the decision-maker. Although the situations have been altered to protect the privacy of individuals, each case tells the story of real people with real problems.

The cases, collected from large and small universities throughout the country, are divided into two general categories. The first part of the book describes the changing campus scene, issues of contention today but not necessarily relevant ten years ago nor ten years in the future. The second part describes the continuing campus scene, the everyday problems of running a university and educating students. Related decisions involving a single issue are grouped into a chapter.

Decisions in Part One focus on such contemporary and disturbing issues as the "new" morality of today's student, institutional relationships with industry, government, and the military, racial problems, and student demands for power. Part Two deals with such issues as When should exceptions to the rules be permitted? What roles do "helping people" play in their contact with students? What information should be released and to whom should it be made available? Ethical standards of professional programs and student protection against faculty tyrants are the subjects of two other chapters. The actual solutions are included for most cases, but the reader is asked to resist the urge to peek until after he has made his own decisions. Relevant questions and issues and suggestions for further involvement with each case are included.

Two chapters have a different emphasis. Chapter 12 discusses several methods for making decisions, shows how each method is useful in certain situations, compares each method, and applies it to one of the troublesome decisions. The author concludes there is no one best method, nor will any single method guarantee good results every time. Some methods are more defensible, however, than others. Chapter 13 consists of fifteen short, personal confrontations in which the reader is asked a question and is expected to answer quickly. The questions are generally awkward to answer and are of the type that arise without warning during a normal day for participants.

MAKING USE OF THE BOOK

A student can increase his knowledge of the problems of higher education simply by reading the decision narratives plus the explanatory material. However, in-depth understanding can be achieved only if readers actually become involved in the decision situations. Creative students can plan their own original use of the material, but three suggestions for involvement are role-playing, fact-finding, and formulating university policy statements.

Role-Playing

Most of the case histories contain plots for several playlets. Each decision is really only one link in a chain of decisions that have preceded and followed the one described in the narrative. Role-playing any aspect of the chain elicits a better understanding of the dynamics and induces, to some degree, the emotions involved in being in a disturbing situation. When a person becomes involved emotionally, he typically reacts with less reason and control. This pattern tends to complicate the matter, and a student can learn how such emotions and reactions influence the outcomes of decisions by actually experiencing such dilemmas. In terms of training, learning to cope with his reactions will help prepare a student to handle similar reactions when they are aroused again in decision situations.

The proper spirit for role-playing is not to make it easy but to make it as difficult as possible for the decision-maker. Role-players should feel free to embellish and challenge each other as they unfold the plot. Complete details of each case are not included in the text and should be added as needed to fit the occasion. For example, one participant may ask another participant an irrelevant question because he cannot think of anything else to ask. The proper response in such circumstances is to improvise an answer without breaking the continuity of the dialogue. Irrelevant questions are quite common. When one class was role-playing The Case of the Nude Dancers in chapter 2, the district attorney asked whether the nude co-ed dancer lived in a dormitory, what she was majoring in, and what year in school she was!

Advance reading of the narrative, consideration of the character of the people in the narrative, preparation for the role-playing, providing a few props and setting at least a minimum stage will produce more realistic results. Occasionally bringing in a stranger and introducing him as the central figure in the case creates reality and excitement.

Role-playing is particularly beneficial when a student tends to empathize with only one side of the problem. To assign him a role on the opposing side will increase his sensitivity toward the difficulties of making decisions which will, in turn, develop a more sympathetic as well as a more competent decision-maker.

Fact-Finding

Fact-finding suggestions are mentioned in the Questions and Issues and the Further Involvement sections that follow each decision case. If the decision deals with admission to professional programs, a reader may wish to find out what admission criteria are used by one or more professional schools. This will increase his knowledge of admissions criteria and, in addition, make him more aware of the problems of using such criteria. If the decision depends on the definition of obscenity, talking with the local police chief to find out how obscenity is defined by law and how those laws are generally enforced on and/or off campus can be useful. If the reader discovers that he has a great deal to learn about campuses, rules, and participants' roles, then this book will have been successful.

Formulating Policy

Formulating university policy statements is the third suggestion for involvement. Good policy statements are difficult to draft, and once drafted, it is generally easy to find fault with them. As an example, there is no rational reason for setting the eighth week of a term as the deadline for dropping courses. But try to frame alternate plans, including a no-deadline policy, that are any easier to defend. You should take the necessary time to try to write adequate statements of policy. If you will actively think through each statement, you will be better able to make a contribution later when you become part of an instructional or administrative staff of a university; and, if your vocation leads to other fields, you will certainly be more sensitive to policy-making problems faced by students, faculty, and administrators in higher education.

The case histories need not be studied in the sequence presented in the book. Surprise is worthy of use. "Real life" participants are often unprepared and off their guard when a problem falls upon them and demands a decision. Trouble does not arrive in an orderly fashion. Suddenly asking a reader to become involved in a case for which he is not prepared increases the troublesomeness of the decision and gives him an increased awareness that there is often no way to plan in advance for every possible problem. Surprise can also be achieved by using a situation from your own experience or by asking others to supply personal troublesome decisions for use later.

There are many creative ideas and activities that can be introduced with these cases. Learning is meant to be fun, interesting, and stimulating. This book is written in that spirit. It is hoped that it will be used that way.

Part One

Today's Troublesome Decisions

1

The Changing Campus

"Damn! Damn, damn, damn! What in the hell were they trying to do?" Professor Johnson muttered to himself. "How is a man supposed to talk above that racket?" He walked over and slammed the window shut. He came back to the lectern, glanced at the students who only half filled the room, and began to lecture again in a louder voice.

It was no use. The closed window did not shut out the noise. "On strike, shut it down; on strike, shut it down"—over and over again, louder and louder. His voice was shot, half his class was gone, and the other half was not listening to him. It had been a bad week. Five days of student protests. Five days of interrupted lectures and dwindling attendance. Five days of chanting, shouting, singing. Should he dismiss class or not? During one of his lectures yesterday, a small group of protesters had marched into the classroom and had tried to take over, shouting him down. Some of his students had joined the protesters, but others had become irate and had attempted to oust them physically. After five solid days of this sort of thing, feelings were running high. He decided not to risk a student clash and told his students to leave.

He picked up his lecture notes and started down the hall to his office. Maybe he could still get a little work done. He turned the corner and saw that his office was blockaded by banner-waving dissidents still chanting, "On strike, shut it down." There was another door; he'd try that way. Professor Johnson turned around and walked down another corridor. He was relieved to find the back door to his office clear of students.

He glanced around and quickly went in, shutting the door behind him. His office, however, was not empty. Several secretaries from other parts of the building had remembered the back door to his office and had taken refuge there, along with his own secretary. They told him it was rumored that things were really bad—much worse than they had been on campus during other disruptions. The girls decided to sneak out a side door, go down a service drive, and around a storage shed to reach the parking lot. Hill Street, in front of the building, was a no-man's-land with pickets, they all assured him. He told them to go ahead and leave; he would lock up and leave later.

"Outrageous," the professor told himself. The noise in the hall was louder. Professor Johnson decided to go home. He filled his briefcase with notes, two folders that were on his desk, and three of his more precious books, and left through the back door, carefully locking it. He told himself he had every right to leave by the front door and to walk home the way he always did, down Hill Street to the other end of the campus. But he didn't. He clenched his heavy briefcase and followed the secretaries' route.

When he reached the parking lot, he looked up toward Hill Street. He could see the mobs of students, almost in a holiday mood, gaily stopping traffic and urging motorists to join them. The gaiety was a veneer, Professor Johnson thought to himself. Five days of semirioting were too much. What if emotions and patience ran out? What if one of those motorists lost his cool, as the students would say, and rammed into the crowded human blockade? This was no way for a university to act. What would people think? What would the legislature, meeting in special session this very day, do? And when could he get back to teaching history?

YESTERDAY AND TODAY

Twenty years ago college professors and administrators could view their lives with satisfaction, equanimity, and occasionally with smugness. Campuses were quiet communities where professors could prepare lectures, read, do research in their fields of interest, isolated and protected from the rush of the outside world. Their relationships with students were characterized by cordial detachment and formally arranged encounters. Students listened or not to their lectures, responded politely and correctly to them, then pursued their own extracurricular activities, careful not to emit noise that might disturb the outsiders. Professors were teachers; students were learners.

Administrators kept the university running by finding and allocating funds and by implementing campus rules which had been established by committees comprised of faculty and administrators. Liaison was established with legislatures, alumni groups, businesses and government agencies to supply the university with finances, to hire graduates, and to take advantage of research facilities. The relationships appeared to be necessary and satisfactory to all concerned.

Today this tranquil setting is an arena, and participants are gladiators, fighting each other while the outside world watches with fascination or horror or vindictiveness. The same professor who twenty years ago lectured to a roomful of semiattentive but polite students is today confronted by students complaining loudly that his material is irrelevant and that the grading system is an arbitrary artifact of history! Twenty years ago a professor who was deemed "unsatisfactory" would have been quietly dismissed after due deliberations by the appropriate dean or faculty committee. Today the very deliberations are interrupted by dissident student groups demanding that the professor be retained. Twenty years ago polished representatives of the corporate world appeared on campus to recruit bright young graduates. Today security forces accompany those representatives in order to hold back protesters during the scheduled interviews.

It takes no seer to perceive that the campus scene is different than it was twenty years ago. It has not changed, however, as much as students would like. The practice of making militant demands for change is the campus way of life. Demonstrations against the "establishment" continue and will continue into the future. The surface turmoil is readily apparent; to trace the turmoil to its cause is extremely difficult.

San Francisco State College has been confronted with disruption and violence almost continuously since 1965. Brigham Young University has had no disruptions. Columbia University, University of Wisconsin—Madison, Duke University, San Fernando Valley State College, University of Massachusetts, St. Cloud State College, Colorado State University, Florida State University, University of California—Berkeley, Bluefield State College, to mention a few, have all seen sporadic disruptions in the last few years. Although this chapter is about the current campus disruptions, the reader must remember that there are far more universities that have had no disruptions than there are those that have. Most universities have not been as affected by the current turmoil as modern methods of communication would have the observer believe. This fact, however, does not detract from the nature of the crises. Even if actual disruption is not all-pervasive, the possibility of disruption is. The future participant in higher education must prepare himself now for decisions he will have to make that will relate to changes being discussed quietly or actively battled for today.

Student demonstrations are not confined to any specific geographical region, type or size of college. On the night of February 13, 1969, a CBS newscaster announced that the National Guard had been called onto the campus of the University of Wisconsin—Madison. He continued by saying that there was police action at Duke University, Durham, North Carolina, and there had been violence at ten other universities that day. The ten were located east, west, south, and north throughout the nation.

Issues have been as varied as have been the institutional targets. A partial list includes dormitory living regulations, free speech, city traffic regulations, new gymnasiums, wages for college maintenance employees, firing of professors, police brutality, amnesty, draft laws, recruiting on campus, hiring black administrators, admission of the disadvantaged, and establishing black studies departments. Many are local issues that arise in response to local conditions. The Cox Commission (1968) and Muscatine Report (1966) describe these respectively at Columbia and at Berkeley. Issues concerning racial opportunity and the war in Vietnam have received major and continued emphasis at many colleges.

During any given demonstration, varying numbers of students are involved. The total tends to be a small percentage of the student body. Demonstrations have been initiated and sustained by as few as twenty or thirty students, but it is fairly common to see a crowd of two to four hundred involved in demonstrating. Four hundred students in a small college of 8,000 is only one out of twenty students. One thousand marchers on a campus the size of the University of Wisconsin is only one out of thirty students; yet those small numbers can mobilize immense power.

Included in the estimates of crowd size are the curious and the sympathizers who are not actively involved. An undetermined number of nonstudents, such as students from other campuses, university dropouts, and local high school students, are also counted. Numbers vary from hour to hour depending on circumstances. The number of demonstrators rises when response to a peaceful demonstration appears to students to be too forceful, when there is obvious justice in the demonstrators' cause, or when there is little conflict between participation in the demonstration and participation in other university activities. During the afternoon of February 13, 1969, about 1,500 students attempted to block entrances to university buildings in Madison, Wisconsin. That night, an exceptionally balmy winter's evening, a crowd of approximately 8,000 to 10,000 marched peacefully out of the campus district, down State Street, and on to the State Capitol grounds.

Actual numbers are relatively unimportant. The ability of a small group to overpower a larger group depends upon the strategy used, the nature of the larger group, and on how the larger group perceives the character and the motives of the smaller group. Several hundred people in South America have seized control of an entire country. Universities, by their very nature and purpose, make it easy for a small group of demonstrators to seize control. Doors are rarely locked. People tend to mind their own business, assuming that others will do the same. If proper plans are made and executed, fifty students can occupy a building.

United Press International released the following article with a January 10, 1969, Waltham, Massachusetts, dateline:

More than 200 white students demonstrated Thursday at Brandeis University and staged a sit-in to support 65 blacks who seized control of the University's communication complex to protest "racist policies."

The students sought amnesty for the blacks who had taken over Ford Hall, a three story classroom building which contains the University's switchboard. The protesting Negroes meanwhile remained barricaded in Ford Hall and the switch-board was closed down.

In this instance, the potency of a small number was increased because other students viewed their cause as a just one and were willing to support it when the occasion warranted. Ending the war in Vietnam, providing a more relevant education for all students, and, especially, obtaining increased educational opportunities for blacks are issues that most students will support.

Regardless of the number of students involved in actual demonstrations, the number of persons who are affected by the disturbance is inevitably large. An accounting of one campus incident will illustrate this. During the first week of February, 1969, about fifty black students on the University of Wisconsin's Madison campus presented the administration with thirteen demands. From this rather inauspicious beginning, a disruption grew so large that 2,000 National Guardsmen were required to keep anywhere from 1,500–8,000 students under control and to keep the university open. Before that, during seven days of sporadic trouble, about 150 university, city, and county policemen were on duty for up to eighteen hours at a time. Firemen, radio dispatchers, and jailers put in extra hours on their own jobs in addition to covering for police officers kept on the campus. Several traffic court judges said that they were unable to hold court for three days because of the lack of available traffic officers to testify. Stopping briefly to see where the count-down is, approximately 2,250 law enforcement people, not normally involved with campus life, have been affected. If their families and business associates are taken into account, we have a conservative figure of 5,000 people at this point.

Several times during the disruption traffic was stopped and buses were taken off routes near the campus area. If 40 people depend on each bus for transportation and a bus drives along that particular route every twenty minutes, about 120 people would be late for work or for an appointment or for a class each hour. And, again, the number must be enlarged because at least one other person would be inconvenienced at the delay or absence of the late bus rider. Now the number of those directly touched by the disruption has become 5,240 at least. Then there are always a few who become involved because they lack the good sense to stay away from the area. Five Madison high school boys, ages fifteen and sixteen, were arrested for shooting a can of oven spray at adults in the sidewalk spectator crowd. All five were referred to their parents and to juvenile court. Two drivers became impatient during a traffic jam near the campus, accelerated their cars and bumped student marchers obstructing the street. The numbers continue to grow, and the people behind each number continue to become more irate and irrational at their condemnation of the disrupters.

It seems safe to say that about 10,000 people, including parents and alumni, were affected by the February disturbance, and this figure does not include the 2,500 faculty members, 400 university and city maintenance men, the other 25,000 students, or the 132 state legislators. When this number of people are inconvenienced, anger and frustration are directed at the university. Twenty years ago the average citizen would probably view "his" state university with some small degree of awe, respect, and reverence. He probably would want to send his progeny to be educated there in order to get a "good" job. He would return to the campus once a year as a pilgrim to recapture for a fleeting moment the memories of his good times on campus. He would look with pride at his name among the financial donors listed in the alumni magazine.

Today, as he watches with horror the anger and violence on the campus, he feels helpless rage. He sees his tax dollars being spent to educate hippie students and to support radical professors. He turns to the only source of influence he knows, his representative in the state legislature. He writes and demands action. An unfortunate result of this chain of events in many states has been the reduction of funds to the universities; and when this has happened, a handful of students, acting out their anger and unhappiness, have damaged the university in a more serious way than by shutting down a building or by picketing the president's office.

The average citizen does not understand the historical reasons for a university or the many ways universities have been changing during the last twenty years. Students are different; they now demand a voice in decisions that affect them. Professors are different; they are in more demand for their skills and knowledge than ever before. Administrators are different. Politicians, goodwill ambassadors, high-powered businessmen, fund raisers— these are the people who direct our universities today. Small wonder that the participant on campus sees himself in the very uncomfortable position of having to make rational decisions that might help someone but that won't direct the wrath of the populace or the students toward him.

Who Are the Dissenters?

Who are these students who demand so much of an older and more experienced world? Where have they come from and why do they act as they do? One group that has been able to get an inordinate amount of publicity is the Students for Democratic Society (SDS) which has chapters on many campuses and has been accused of being the guiding force behind recent disruptions. At Columbia University it was identified as an active group calling for unacceptable reforms. The leader of the SDS during the April, 1968, rebellion at Columbia was a student named Mark Rudd who made the demands in the name of the organization. As spokesman for several groups, Rudd attacked the administration in a most abusive manner. He led the resistance when faculty and administrators made attempts to obtain peaceful solutions to student protests. Although many people think radical groups such as SDS and their leaders plan, implement, and control the course of revolutionary demonstrations, the Cox Commission concluded otherwise from its study of the Columbia disturbance.

The Cox Commission (1968) reports that, at Columbia at least, the SDS is not a cohesive group but is several subgroups supporting different philosophies. The Commission writes of the "tension between those who wanted to concentrate on public education and internal organization and those who stressed protest demonstration. . . . College seniors in SDS even spoke of the 'generation gap' that separated them from sophomore members." The report estimates that there were 50 to 100 members and cites evidence that there was a great gulf between what SDS planned and what actually happened. At moments of crisis, other persons provided leadership. Much of the violence was due to local unhappiness, inept administrative action, and impromptu faculty responses.

The position that SDS is neither stable nor consistent is supported by Kenniston (Hall, 1968) and more recently by the actions of SDS members. At the SDS annual convention in Chicago, August, 1969, one group of members seceded to form a new radical organization.

The Society for Afro-American Students (SAS), a black radical group, also gained national notoriety during the April, 1969, Columbia disturbance. The Cox Commission concluded that although the SAS played an insignificant role in the events leading to the uprising, it was much more disciplined and cohesive than was the SDS. After students, black and white, had "captured" Hamilton Hall, SAS members demanded that white students leave the building and take their own hall. This challenge precipitated more building takeovers. When police entered the fracas, however, SAS members submitted to arrest with no violence, in contrast to the fight put up by white students in other buildings.

During October, 1967, the University of Wisconsin had the most violent disruption in its history to that time. The two groups most active in the incident were the University Community Action group and the Anti-Dow Coordinating Committee. Neither of these groups appeared at the Columbia riots seven months later; neither was the SDS in evidence during the Dow demonstration in Madison. It is interesting to note that neither of these two groups, the University Community Action group nor the Anti-Dow Committee, played a significant part in the February, 1969, demonstration on the Wisconsin campus. Most of the political-community structures that students build are not the traditional party-service club structures of "straight" society.

Student coalitions spring up, serve a purpose, and vanish as new ones rise up to replace them.

The February, 1969, Wisconsin riot was initiated by demands of the Black Peoples Alliance, but this small group was rapidly joined by others. During the days preceding the demonstration, many groups of students acted independently in support of widely divergent causes. The Sociology Students Association was harassing the sociology department because it had not re-hired a popular professor. The English Students Association was actively trying to get a voice in English department affairs and had interrupted de-partmental faculty meetings. The Teaching Assistants Association (TAA) had polled its membership and was threatening a strike because of an im-pending bill in the legislature that would reduce the income of out-of-state teaching assistants. Other groups contributing to the turmoil were the History Students Association, Philosophy Students Association, SDS, Black Council, United Front, Third World Federation, Wisconsin Alliance, and the Draft Resistance Union. Although each acted independently at times, about 8,000-10,000 banded together for the massive, peaceful march the evening of Feb-ruary 13. When faced with this shifting quicksand of persons, groups, and causes, an administrator may be unnerved. "Whom am I dealing with? How many do you represent? How were you selected? Will you keep your agree-ments?" Usually he gets no satisfactory answer to any of these questions.

Demonstrations are more likely to be understandable in terms of com-mon characteristics of individuals than in organized group activity. Some of the differences between activist and nonactivist students are summarized in the Muscatine Report (1966). The report notes that social science and humanities majors were most numerous among students arrested at Sproul Hall on the Berkeley campus on December 2 and 3, 1964. The professions such as law, electrical engineering, and education were far less in evidence; and agriculture, forestry, optometry, and public health were not represented at all. The arrested students had significantly higher grades than those of nonactivist students. The report also shows that support for the demonstra-tion was greater among those with high grade-point averages than among those with low averages. In addition, there was greater support among those living off campus than among those living on campus.

Additional information on the characteristics of activists is given by Flacks (1967). He found activists to be more creative and less concerned with status, conventional morality, and religion than nonactivists. Flacks claims that activists and their parents are strongly characterized by two clusters of humanistic values. He identifies the first cluster as individual de-velopment, self-expression, and spontaneous expression. The second cluster he sees as ethical humanism, concern for the social condition of others. Flacks maintains that the locus of the difference between activists and others is the matter of self-expression versus the dominant societal value of self-control.

The activists that Flacks studied tend to come from urban professional, upper-status families that are highly educated and more liberal than other families of the same status. Flacks concludes that such students have not chosen to rebel in the usual sense but are actually fulfilling an already established familial trend which is at odds with the dominant American culture. Recent research reported by Kerpelman (1969) and by Watts, Lynch, and Whittaker (1969) supports the idea that student activists come from more highly educated liberal families where the parents encourage the social protest philosophy of their offspring.

It should be noted that the most recent trend is for black and third-world students to organize independently. The characteristics of such students may or may not be similar to their white counterparts.

While demonstrations are mainly organized and supported by bright, highly advantaged humanists, it would be unrealistic to suppose that the mob does not gather others as well: the emotionally upset, the camp followers, those who are bored and seeking excitement, those who have never been in a riot before and would like to see what it is like, a few anarchists, and several who have had too many beers.

Demonstrations are often related to appealing causes, but just as often the means of the demonstration makes no sense to most observers. It is difficult to understand how throwing an egg at a national draft official as he delivers a speech can alter the course of the war in Vietnam or change the draft laws. It is difficult to understand how preventing college placement interviews can affect the government's decision to use napalm in Vietnam. It is difficult to understand why a university should be accused of racism simply because it holds stock in a particular American bank. It is difficult to understand how a group can send a nonnegotiable demand to a university about a financial matter over which the university has no control and then demand that the university be shut down because it does not comply. It is difficult to understand why a napalm manufacturer should cause a massive demonstration in October, 1967, but not rate a single picket on the same campus in February, 1969. Each situation mentioned has actually occurred. Yet many seem pointless if the goal of action is to change conditions.

There are even more basic ways in which the protest movement is irrational. Four paradoxes are described by Rubinstein (1969): (1) In the very effort to uphold their individual freedom, the student activists forcibly abridge the freedom of others. (2) The 'dogmatic antidogmatism' of their pronouncements. Activists believe they are right and can exclude from consideration any other viewpoint, even while criticizing those who do hold the other point of view for being dogmatic. (3) Activists reject present political ways of running society but engage vociferously in their own brand of politics. (4) Rubinstein labels the fourth paradox "no matter what you do you can't win." This amounts to a struggle to find a basis for confrontation no matter how permissive the environment.

The appearance of violence on the campus is only one of the many changes on college campuses. Entering freshmen are better educated than they ever were before. They tend to be more adamant and more vocal about what they believe is right. They have developed more liberal morals, new ethical systems, and are more likely to have experimented with drugs. Universities have grown much larger and, as a result, have split into departments, schools, and so on, each vying for its own special interests. Faculty are expected to do their fair share of work on committees, which results in removing the teachers even farther from students. Students complain about the faceless institution and the feeling that humanity has flown leaving machines and assistants in charge.

Faculty are in constant demand as consultants to business, government, and other colleges. They are far more mobile than ever before, and this increases the lack of continuity of exposure that a student can have with one faculty member. Also, more faculty members are writing and conducting research than before, but students and legislatures are questioning the need for much of it. New and different kinds of colleges, such as two-year colleges and experimental schools, have come into being. As numbers of students and faculty increase, campuses have had to expand physically, creating problems in neighboring areas.

Growing pains, changes in social values, and increased technology certainly have contributed to the problems facing participants in higher education. With this brief overview of the changing scene, we pass to the more detailed description of some very interesting decisions that serve to illustrate and pinpoint crucial issues. As these case studies are read, other aspects of the changing scene and its traumatic impact on individuals will become more apparent.

2

Student Morality

Twenty years ago freshman co-eds arrived on campus, checked into a supervised housing unit, and thereafter were guarded and watched over by a housemother. Co-eds had hours to keep and regulations about when and where they could visit with members of the opposite sex. The university was thought to have the same responsibilities as those of parents.

"Good" girls did not become involved sexually while at college or, for that matter, anywhere else prior to their marriage. The girl who did allow herself to become involved kept such involvement quiet. Twenty years ago "The Arrangement" was not considered an acceptable mode of living by parents, college authorities, or even by many students themselves. As the reader knows, things have changed. The first case history reflects new attitudes regarding sex and the problems it brings to institutions which have not fully accepted the changing morality and are not quite sure if their faculty, alumni, and others would approve of such change.

THE ARRANGEMENT

Foreword: You are one of a three-member campus judiciary committee which recommends the disciplinary action to be taken by the dean of student affairs against students found guilty of violating college regulations.

Decision Problem: You and the other members of the committee are meeting in a conference room on campus. Seated across the table from you is Linda, a sophomore co-ed, charged with a housing violation. The committee chairman calls the hearing to order.

"It has been brought to the attention of this committee," he says, glancing around the table, "that Linda Roberts and Paul Smith are living together in an off-campus apartment. College rules state that co-eds under twenty-one must live in supervised housing or with a relative." The chairman pauses

17

and takes a document out of a folder. He continues, "I have here Linda's housing application on which she stated she was living at the given address with an aunt. As you all know, a recent article in the college newspaper quoted Linda as saying she was living off campus with a male companion. Linda, do you have anything to say about the charges against you?"

Linda looks directly at the chairman and agrees that the facts as stated are true, but she claims they are not the issue at all. She says that the university has no right to police student morals, and she attacks the school and committee members for their failure to understand changing moral values, for upholding antiquated, repressive rules, and for trying to impose jurisdiction where they have no right to do so. She says that she lived in a dorm her freshman year, started going with Paul, and during the summer moved into an apartment with him. She concludes by asserting that other couples are also living together off campus, that the student newspaper is supporting her cause, and that "freedom committees" have formed to help fight the "Victorian and inappropriate" regulation. She tells the committee that she is making an issue of the rule and will appeal any disciplinary action taken against her.

You and the other committee members question her, trying to return to the housing policy and Linda's violations. But Linda sees these as mere technicalities and sticks to her basic arguments concerning student rights in nonacademic matters.

The chairman realizes nothing new is being discussed and dismisses Linda. As background information, the chairman tells you that the dean of women had talked privately to Linda and had agreed to drop the matter if Linda moved back into a dorm. Linda refused. The chairman also states that Linda's parents know she is living with Paul and do not object. Her parents do not know, however, that she falsified residency information.

Making the Decision:
You know some influential alumni have stated that the university should continue to supervise and regulate housing arrangements for undergraduate female students. You know there is a state law covering fornication and that spokesmen for the university have stated that the school will not encourage violation of state laws. You are also aware of new student ideas about morality and an increasingly permissive attitude by the university toward nonacademic student concerns. You think that to have a rule and not enforce it creates a climate of inconsistency which is not conducive to attaining academic goals. Finally, you know there is great interest in the decision and

that the committee's recommendation will become public knowledge.

The alternatives before you range from doing nothing, to giving a verbal reprimand, to suspending Linda from the university.

Your Decision:
As a member of the committee, what disciplinary action are you going to recommend?

STOP! Make your decision before proceeding.

Questions and Issues:
1. In what nonacademic areas do colleges have a right to govern activities of students? How does a college answer this question? (Before you tackle these, see if you can get a copy of the charter or enabling legislation of your college.)
2. What rules governing nonacademic matters should colleges establish? How does a college answer this question?
3. To what extent should students be involved in determining such rules?
4. How should such rules be enforced? What part should students play in this enforcement?
5. What effect does publicity and strong divergent public opinion have on a committee decision?
6. Under what conditions is supplying false information to conceal a rule violation justified?

Further Involvement:
1. Obtain a copy of housing regulations. Find out how such regulations are enforced. Suggest modifications. Obtain a copy of rules and regulations that apply to sexual conduct and to off-campus activities of students. Suggest modifications.
2. Role-play Linda's confrontation with the committee. Then have the committee consider the issues.

What Actually Happened:
Linda was found guilty of violating the housing regulations and of falsifying statements about her place of residence. As punishment, her campus social and extracurricular activities were restricted, and she was ordered to change her living arrangements.

By the time the hearing and an appeal ended, spring term was over, so the punishment was of little consequence to Linda. She and her boyfriend left town saying they would return in the fall, but they did not.

The university did not try to determine identities of the other couples who were supposedly living together. It was hoped the matter would be forgotten. Housing regulations were subsequently modified so that a girl could live off campus with parental permission.

FOUR-LETTER WORDS

The "new morality" has had great impact upon language. Most people have heard or read the majority of four-letter words used to describe sex acts, various parts of the anatomy, and functions of the body in eliminating waste. Twenty years ago most books and newspapers did not print them, either bowdlerizing the offending passages or carefully inserting blank letters. Today students are following the lead of novelists and playwrights and are including *all* words in their writing and speaking. The so-called free-speech movement at Berkeley was one well-publicized example of this. There, students made free speech a major issue and the results were arrests, suspensions, and bitterness. In less publicized and less violent incidents, the forbidden-word issue has been raised on other campuses. Suppose you are the faculty advisor to the student newspaper and the following series of events occur.

Decision Problem: The campus newspaper has become more adventuresome in its use of four-letter words, viewed by many as "naughty." Alumni and legislators are saying that such words should not be in print in any form, especially not in a campus newspaper. The words, however, are in print in many famous novels, and the courts have held that such words are not in themselves obscene, so the campus editor argues that his writers have a legal right to use them. He points out that they are not used to shock but are used only when they best describe the situation. He makes the claim that artistic integrity is involved and that he would not be true to his profession if he censored articles.

You tell him that several members of the legislature have stated that no campus newspaper should be printing such words. The student editor answers by saying that he will continue to print them and he will not resign.

Making the Decision: What are you going to do now? You could recommend that he be fired. You could recommend that the paper be censored before it is published. You could recommend that writers of the articles be suspended from school. You could resign.

Your Decision: What are you going to do? As university representative to the paper, central administration expects you either to do something or to recommend some procedure.

STOP! Make your decision before proceeding.

Questions and Issues:
1. What is appropriate speech in the classroom? in the press?
2. Does a professor or administrator have any right to limit speech? If so, how?
3. If printed matter written by students does not violate state or federal laws, does the university have any right to discipline the writer or require prior approval before publication?
4. On what basis can university intervention be justified?

Further Involvement:
1. Determine the editorial policies and administrative structure of your campus newspaper. Find out how the policies are formulated. Comment on their adequacy.
2. Find out if there is a safeguard for control in the event the newspaper ceases to report objectively and becomes a propaganda machine. Should there be such a safeguard?
3. Is there a limit beyond which spoken or written speech should not go? Experiment in class and see to what extent there is agreement on this matter. If some feel there is a limit, how do you define the limit?

What Actually Happened: The advisor repeated the editor's declaration to the administration. He said he could do nothing because he had no authority to fire the editor who was elected each year. He stated that he respected the editor's position and that if anything were to be done about the situation, it would have to come from someone higher up. He added that the trustees, alumni, and others were kidding themselves if they thought they could effectively stop such words from reaching the eyes of the undergraduate population. To document this position he brought along a copy of the campus underground paper which was sold on the street outside each campus entrance once a week. The advisor recommended the subject be dropped.

The subject was not dropped, however. The trustees asked the editor to appear before them for questioning. He refused. The advisor resigned. At the time of this writing, the paper was continuing its policy; the trustees were considering possible action for the future.

THE CASE OF THE NUDE DANCERS

Changes in permissible language have been accompanied by changes
in acceptable minimal standards of exposure of the human body. Judges have
ruled that motion pictures may be shown that were banned ten years ago.
Bathing suits are increasingly briefer; topless and bottomless dancers have
been legalized in California. While the changes are widespread, they have not
been universally accepted. In many states such a dancer is subject to immediate arrest. Certainly universities have not officially legalized any variation or
deviation of dress that the whole community has not yet accepted. If a student-initiated play which presents nude dancing is performed in a community where such dancing is not allowed, university officials find themselves in trouble.

**Decision
Problem:**   Student drama groups delight in exploring unconventional
modes of expression. Recently, one bright, young, would-be
producer decided to stage a modern version of *Peter Pan,* a
well-known children's play. After considerable rehearsal, it
was premiered in the student union on university property and
was attended only by students. This morning, in spite of the
restricted audience, the local newspaper blared into every home
the news that nude co-eds danced in the play. Immediately public protest zeroes in on the university.

The community considers the district attorney to be the
guardian of local morals, and it is his job to determine if the
play is obscene according to law. He has not seen the performance, he cannot find anyone who will admit to having seen it,
and he cannot find anyone who will identify the alleged nudes.
No member of the faculty or administration has seen the play,
so they will not state whether or not it is obscene. However,
they do issue a statement saying that even if they had seen the
play, they would make no judgment because obscenity is a
legal matter.

The students react as rapidly as the public, rallying to
cries of freedom of expression, artistic integrity, and community
meddling in student affairs. They say the play did not offend
the student audience and that it should not be judged by community standards. They claim that neither the university nor
the district attorney has any right to interfere.

No one actually knows whether the play violates a state or
local law. The adult community is not ready for public nudity.
The state legislature and the governing body of the university
are not ready for public nudity. Students, however, support
the right of artists to produce a play with nudity especially when

it is an essential, artistic part of the play. Civil libertarians are concerned that the dancers' or the producer's rights will be abridged.

Making the Decision: According to the spirit of the day, the producer defiantly states that he is scheduling the next performance in the same student union two nights from today. The district attorney promptly replies that if the play is performed and if there is nude dancing, he will act to cause the arrests, on an obscenity charge, of the dancers and the producer.

Many people are faced with decisions. In anticipation of this performance, assume you are each of the following people. Indicate what you are going to do.

Your Decision: Director of the union:

Dean of student affairs:

President of the university:

District attorney:

A member of the governing body of the university:

Faculty advisor to the play:

A member of the cast who does not dance:

STOP! Make your decisions before proceeding.

Questions and Issues: 1. Is a university a part of the larger community or is it an entity in matters pertaining to obscenity, free speech, and morals? Do you think it should be separated from the community?
2. Should a city official be allowed to come into a university campus to arrest a person whom the university itself has not accused of illegal action?
3. Is a state university obligated to enforce the state and local statutes that pertain to such things as obscenity?

Further Involvement: 1. Discuss problems involved in defining and enforcing laws related to obscenity.
2. Interview a sample of students and townspeople about what should be allowed in campus drama productions. Include questions in the interview about words, actions, and exposure.
3. Role-play a dialogue between the producer of the play, the university president, and the district attorney.

What Actually Happened:

A private showing for the people most involved was arranged. The district attorney attended, left, and ruled the performance obscene. A notice was read to the entire cast, informing them of the ruling and the possibility of arrest if the play was performed again. The university administration immediately ruled that since the play violated the law, the student union could not be used for a performance. Students were irate that "nonstudent" standards should be imposed on them, and the rumor was spread that a surprise performance of the play would be given within a few days.

Making a Subsequent Decision:

Again, assume that you are each of the decision-makers just mentioned. What are you going to do now, if anything? Specifically, are you going to try to stop any future performance? Are you going to try to change the views of any of the people involved? Are you going to intervene in any way? Now assume you are an assistant dean of student affairs who has been told where and when the performance will be held. What are you going to do?

STOP! Make your decision before proceeding.

What Actually Happened Next:

The play was performed on campus in a small auditorium that had been reserved by another student group for a different purpose. Again the local paper used the story as front-page material the next morning, and the barrage of accusations, explanations, and statements started all over again. The city accused the university of condoning an illegal and immoral action. The university answered by saying it did not have information in advance to prevent the performance. The district attorney asked the university for names of the violators, but university officials did not produce them. The community accused them of noncooperation. The university said they did not know who the students were and could get no one to identify them. The district attorney's office tried to uncover the names and to find someone who would appear against the violators, but was unsuccessful. No convictions were ever obtained.

Statements continued to appear in newspapers throughout the state. One prominent man wrote, "Taxpayers do not like to see their tax money go to support purveyors of obscenity." Another attacked the university by writing about "advocates of sexual orgies." And so the controversy continued. Participants received letters and telephone calls for several months after the incident occurred, although the play

was not performed again. Many months later, the moral character of the producer again became a public issue when he applied to the city council for a theater license.

THE SUSPECTED "POT" PUSHER

Twenty years ago if someone were picked up on a drug charge, he was
probably a jazz musician or a derelict of society. Here, too, the scene has
changed. Among the college set LSD gradually has become acceptable.
Timothy Leary, an ex-Harvard professor and the high priest of drugs, has
travelled from campus to campus praising LSD and seeking converts to his
"turned on" way of life. If you were president of a small college in the Midwest, what would you say to a group of students who asked to bring Mr.
Leary to your campus to speak?

The number of students following Leary's lead is dropping, probably
because it is now known that LSD produces harmful effects, but marijuana,
or "pot," has taken its place. Evidence concerning harmful effects from taking
pot is inconclusive, but as of this writing, it is illegal to smoke pot, and a
majority of society believe that marijuana constitutes a menace. On many
campuses, however, a large number of students do smoke pot and see nothing
wrong with it.

Decision
Problem:
Gregg, a sophomore living off campus, has been spending time in his former university residence hall. The housefellow has come to you, a professor friend, for advice because
he thinks Gregg is pushing marijuana to freshmen in the house.
The housefellow has no proof but thinks he knows Gregg well
enough to be fairly sure he is exerting an undue and unhealthy
influence on the freshmen.

The housefellow tells you that he found in the den a number of artifacts usually associated with the use of pot and that
Gregg and the boys he was visiting were in the den that night.
He also tells you that some boys have reported being at pot
parties in Gregg's off-campus residence.

The housefellow asks you what he should do about the
apparent pot-smoking in the dorm and what he should do about
the students he suspects of using the stuff. He also wants to
know what he can do about Gregg's frequent appearances that
seem to be tied in with the smoking.

Your
Decision:
As faculty friend, what will you advise your housefellow
friend to do in this situation? He is obviously concerned about
the boys in his dorm, but he hesitates to take definite action

toward notifying authorities. If you advise him to report his suspicions, which authority will you suggest he contact?

STOP! Make your decision before proceeding.

Questions and Issues:
1. Do you feel that individuals have a right to smoke pot in the privacy of their room? Does it make any difference if that room is in a private home or a university dorm?
2. What should a university do to punish students who smoke pot off campus? On campus in a dorm?
3. What is the appropriate role of a housefellow in a case where he knows a dormitory student is violating a university regulation?
4. What should a university do, if anything, to keep the use of pot from spreading? Are new freshmen entitled to some protection from those who would sell or give them pot?

Further Involvement:
Role-play the scene between the professor and the housefellow.

What Actually Happened:
The professor friend advised the housefellow to report the matter to his superior, which he did. Part of the problem in this case was that both the professor and the housefellow thought laws concerning marijuana should be altered to make its use legal.

Another Pot Problem Example:
Another "pot case" pertains to a girl whose roommate in the dorm smokes pot. The girl does not like it, and since her roommate is very careless, she is sure the situation will be discovered. The girl wants to change roommates, but doesn't know how to broach the subject to the head resident whose approval she needs. She doesn't want to get her roommate into trouble, but she is not able to study and feels a change is essential. Discuss how you think she should proceed.

3

Institutional Morality

Until fairly recent times the typical university student was primarily concerned with preparing himself to make money after graduation, and his involvement with problems of the outside world was in the form of philosophical discussions of political and economic cures for the more obvious ills. Today's student tends to be an activist as well as an idealist. He is questioning the way society is conducting its affairs and preparing for the future.

He attacks the establishment on campus with as many embarrassing accusations as he does the establishment off campus. His rhetoric often becomes a substitute for logic. He does not view the establishment's ethical morality in the same liberal context that he sees his own personal morality. This is not the paradox it appears to be to the casual observer. Today's student sees his own morals as an expression of freedom of self that does not adversely affect another person. At the same time, he is questioning what he thinks are conflicts of interest among the rulers of his world whom he sees as being directly responsible for the suffering of others.

Universities are being forced into soul-searching by students asking these questions: Is the university an isolated bastion for those who "seek the truth" or does it have an obligation to use its vast resources to confront and remedy social evils? Should universities accept money for research facilities from government agencies or industry? Do faculty members have the right to perform duties for industry and government? What obligations do regents and university administrators have to the university community? Is university prestige ever worth a compromise? Who should make decisions pertaining to these questions—faculty, administrators, governing bodies, students? In this chapter we shall examine these questions as they have been asked by real students in real settings.

Traditionally, universities have had difficulty providing adequate research facilities. The costs have been enormous. A valuable source of revenue over the years has been foundational, industrial, and governmental grants to establish research centers and to pay salaries of researchers who, incidentally,

27

teach students. Relationships between grant givers and grant receivers are sometimes clear-cut; other times they are exceedingly complex; but either way they are often viewed by students as unhealthy symptoms of university impurity.

As an interesting example, consider the case of Columbia University and the Strickman Filter. Robert Strickman, an inventor who had no connection with Columbia, claimed to have perfected a cigarette filter that would greatly reduce the risk of cancer from smoking. Mr. Strickman offered to share the profits from the sale of his filter with Columbia in return for the use of its name. The Board of Trustees considered the matter as a business venture and a potentially profitable one for Columbia. An observant press broke the story when many questions concerning the effectiveness of the filter, the ethical issues, and the relationship of the university to the filter were not answered. The controversy that followed the announcement seriously weakened the faith of students and others in the integrity of a great university and forced the question, Should an educational institution enter into a strictly business arrangement?

More subtle examples of financial cooperation between government or private industry and universities abound. Institutes bearing such respected names as the Center for Theoretical Physics have been awarded research contracts by one of the armed services or by the Institute for Defense Analysis (IDA). The IDA was established by the Department of Defense to obtain university research and counsel about military matters.

These research contracts are not generally publicized. The exact nature of the research or the service performed to the military is not known nor is it easily available. That the university has not revealed the information about such research contracts makes it vulnerable, a likely target for student protesters.

Usually research contracts directly benefit universities, enabling them to hire more competent faculty and build better facilities for instruction. The contracts may result in significant new contributions to science. The motives of the professors may be pure and scientific. But students sometimes ignore these valuable by-products and focus on the fact that they are produced by "tainted money" from the military-industrial complex. The Cox Commission reports that this issue was one that contributed to the uprising at Columbia in the spring of 1968.

University ROTC exemplifies a nonmoney facet of conflict of interest for many idealists. According to them, universities are aiding the military in preparations for war. On many campuses ROTC has been the target of protesters, and in some instances it has been eliminated or is being phased out because of protest pressure. Harvard faculty voted to phase out ROTC over a three-year period. At the University of Wisconsin—Madison, Army, Navy, and Air Force ROTC programs have been voluntary since 1960; and since the fall of 1969, ROTC freshman orientation sessions have been voluntary at least partly as the result of student demands. The Army has selected eleven campuses to experiment with a new ROTC program to be taught almost exclusively by civilians as a compromise to ease student objections.

One interesting sidelight to the many varieties of protest against the military in the 1960s is that cooperative efforts between the military and universities have, if anything, decreased since the 1940s. Protests are heard now because students are more interested in and more concerned about immoral wars, governmental interference in personal lives, questionable business methods, and the like.

Another example of university conflict of interest is the purely physical problem of university expansion. As enrollments increase, colleges have to buy land to build more buildings, and if the campus is located in a city, this often means people must be evicted, houses demolished, park and playground areas usurped for university use. "Land condemnation for university expansion in urban areas is an immoral act of a corrupt society," shout the challengers. Expansion problems at Columbia became the Morningside Park issue which was an important factor leading to trouble during the spring of 1968.

Because of a multitude of similar conflict-of-interest charges, some students have concluded that the university is more motivated by money, expansion, and prestige than in searching for truth or helping humanity. They say the university fosters societal evils and is part of a huge racist-government-business-military complex which must be challenged and resisted. When this kind of activist logic prevails, it easily follows that there will be trouble when a company that makes products used by military forces in Vietnam wishes to come onto a campus to recruit college graduates.

THE PERILOUS JOB INTERVIEW DECISION

Decision Problem: The president of the university was listening to the spokesman for a group of seniors who had come to his office to warn him not to let Company X use a campus building for job recruitment.

"The function of the university is to search for truth," the spokesman said, "and it should not allow private industry to use the campus for recruitment. The university has been reduced to a tool of industry."

The spokesman justified their demands by citing the fact that Company X manufactured war materials which were particularly offensive to peace-loving citizens. He continued to explain that the business enterprise of some companies could be tolerated, but the immorality of Company X was so obvious that the university was obligated to protest its evil existence in every possible way.

Members of the group added that although demonstrations had been peaceful at interviews held on the campus earlier in the year, there would be an all-out effort by students to stop the interviews of Company X. They warned that there would be bloodshed if city police were called in. The president was also told there was no organized protest group and no leader, but that each student was acting as an individual citizen.

Your Decision: After the students left his office, the president sat thinking. The interview date given Company X was two weeks away. The president had only a few days in which to decide whether to confirm or to cancel the date with Company X. If you were the president, what would your decision be?

STOP! Make your decision before proceeding.

Questions and Issues:
1. What conditions should be placed on job interviews and recruitment practices by businesses on college campuses?
2. What materials, publicity, rooms, expenses should be handled by the university? By the company?
3. Do students have a right to be interviewed? What force is justifiable to see that they do have the right?
4. Who should make the decision about allowing job interviews—student committees, faculty, or administration?

Further Involvement:
1. Role-play the original confrontation between president and students. Have several students threatening while others push closer, angrily condemning the university for its complicity with the war in Vietnam.
2. Write an interview and placement policy for a university.

What Actually Happened: Authorities on at least four campuses had to make decisions relating to this issue. One university administration made a two-part decision: (1) Communicate and discuss differences with the dissidents to convince them not to carry out their threat of violence; (2) Hold the interviews as scheduled and call in police if necessary, but officials hoped the threat of arrest would stop many students from disrupting activities.

The decision did not produce the desired results. While the interviews were in progress, dissenting students prevented other students from being interviewed and then proceeded to block halls so students could not attend classes. Police were called, and using a loud-speaker system, they asked students to disband. The crowd did not disperse. Instead, students began fighting with police who retaliated with tear gas.

Early reaction to the day's events was dismay that police had been called onto the campus. A substantial number of faculty were critical of this decision. At this point, university administration formed faculty committees to outline responses that the university might use in the future to prevent or to control violence and to develop a policy concerning all placement interviews held on the campus.

Administrators on another campus studied the outcome at the first university and decided to postpone interviews in order to avoid bloodshed. This primary goal was achieved, but students continued to use the same threat over related issues, gaining a series of victories. Now faculty and alumni have become critical of the administration, and the issue is still not resolved.

Making a Subsequent Decision: Interestingly enough, the administration of the first school faced the same decision one year later when Company X again requested an interview date. Now, as the decision-maker, what would you do? Remember, a violent confrontation took place just one year ago.

STOP! Make your decision before proceeding.

What Actually Happened: Essentially the same decision was made except for two important details. (1) The place and time of the interview were changed so crowds would be easier to handle and innocent bystanders would not get hurt. (2) Enough police were there in advance to control any attempts at violence. Interviews were conducted very quietly on a Saturday morning in the Field House while a few pickets walked peacefully back and forth in front of the entrance. Interviews were held on the third anniversary of the original confrontation without so much as a murmer.

THE RETURNED DIPLOMA

There is no doubt that some people feel very deeply about the evil of the war in Vietnam and about the universities' apparent complicity with the war effort. This letter did not really create a difficult decision problem for a university official, but it did force him to do some serious soul-searching as he drafted a reply.

Dear Sir:

     I am returning my diploma and refusing my Master's Degree in Philosophy. In recent years the university has been acting in ways that are incompatible with Christianity, humanitarianism, and peace. Specifically the university helps the military recruit for inhumane actions against the Vietnamese. The university helps the Galt Chemical Company and the Doe Arms Company recruit persons who will be aiding in the making of war material which will be used to kill and maim. The university has done nothing to show its support of peace and love for fellow man.

     My identity as a human being and my integrity as a peace loving citizen cry out and I cannot in all honesty stand to be identified with such an institution. I hope that others will reflect on the meaning of life and the urgency of peace and likewise say "no" to an institution which will not speak out against the inhumanity and injustice of war.

                             Sincerely,

                             Philip Jackson

Your Decision: Write your reply to this alumnus.

STOP! Make your decision before proceeding.

Questions and Issues: 1. Should the university take a stand on moral or ethical issues such as the war in Vietnam, drugs, tobacco?

What Actually Happened: The appropriate administrator drafted the following letter.

Dear Mr. Jackson:

It is with sincere regrets that I note the return of your diploma for the Master's Degree in philosophy. Even though the years of hard work and dedication cannot be undone, it must have taken some deep soul-searching for you to make such a gesture of displeasure with this university. With your permission, I will hold your diploma until such time as your faith and respect may be restored.

In your rush to condemn the university for its role in the Galt incident, I think you may have overlooked the great division that exists here on the subject of

war-related activities. The debate over the reaction
to the demonstration tore at the very heartstrings of
this university and continues to this day. You could
hardly say we are indifferent.

If an institution can be said to have a conscience, its
conscience is the many-faceted collectivity of faculty,
staff, and administration that make up the whole.
When this conscience speaks through its various
committees and boards as it has on the question of
recruiting and disciplining of demonstrators, it is not
because it approves of napalming women and children,
or of war itself, or of repressing freedom of speech;
but because a genuine soul-searching no less valid than
yours has led it to conclude that the ideal is being
served. Which conclusions will stand the test of time
neither of us can tell.

Certainly, Christian morality and the human spirit are
elusive qualities which have evaded man since the
beginning of time, and which over the centuries have
always emblazoned the banners of opposing armies. I
hope we can look forward to a time when the values that
men subscribe to universally reject war, the instruments
of war, and the compromise of freedom.

Sincerely,

John Dix, Dean of Students

THE TRUSTEE'S CONFLICT OF INTEREST

A university community includes many individuals, some of whom have
other interests. Occasionally it appears that these other interests take prece-
dence over the person's university interests or that he may be able to use one
to help the other. In such a case, possible economic gains at the expense of
the university make it appear as if the men who direct the destiny of the university are not as objective as they should be.

Decision Problem: The university president is listening to the Student Association president as he says, "There is clearly a conflict of interest
in the case of Trustee White. He is on the University Board of
Trustees and on the Board of Directors of National Trust which
owns the Chapman Building and leases it to the university.

"The Student Association wrote the local newspaper
which published the facts of the case, and we have a resolution
asking that Mr. White sever his connections either with the
university or with National Trust. We've got the facts in this

matter, and it's a clear-cut conflict of interest. I've even gone to the chairman of the University Board of Trustees, but his secretary always tells me he's busy.

"We're getting some faculty support and something's got to be done, but we're just not getting action. We believe you're the man who can do it, and we think you have a moral obligation to see that this matter is considered at the appropriate level."

Your Decision: As president of the university, what are you going to do about Trustee White?

STOP! Make your decision before proceeding.

Questions and Issues:

1. Do you think Trustee White's situation is a case of conflict of interest?
2. How can one determine when a conflict of interest situation exists?
3. What problems do you foresee in a policy stating that all regents, trustees, and administrators must sell property or stock in companies with whom the university is likely to deal?

What Actually Happened: The president discussed the matter with Trustee White, but the conversation was not made public. When a reporter questioned him, Trustee White said he had nothing to hide because there was no conflict of interest that was in any way detrimental to the welfare of the university.

The Student Association continued its fact-finding and learned that Trustee White's nephew owned property on the fringe of the university and that the property was among several pieces the university wished to buy for expansion.

The Student Association continued to maintain that Trustee White was involved in a conflict-of-interest situation and should resign. Trustee White said that his nephew had owned the property before the university had considered expansion in that area and that he would not resign simply because some students thought he should.

THE SEARCH FOR MONEY

Running a good university is a very expensive business. All institutions that are solvent have perfected ways of making money. Wealthy alumni and friends are solicited, and their gifts make up the difference between regular revenue, such as tuition and appropriations, and costs. Without substantial contributions from outside sources, the modern university could not continue to function at its present level. What kind of money should it take? How should the money be invested? How should funds be managed?

Decision Problem: Several years ago the Board of Trustees purchased 500 shares of stock in a bank. The bank recently loaned money to a company that has few Negroes on its payroll. Civil rights organizations claim the company is prejudiced, and the company denies the charge. Black students at the university are now demanding that the trustees sell the bank stock. They also want the trustees to put this item on their agenda, open the meeting to the public, and change the meeting place so that the 200 blacks on campus may attend and present their case.

About 80 blacks agreed to include the matter on the agenda and to change the location of the meeting. About 80 blacks showed up and about 400 whites jammed the corridors and sat on the front steps of the building chanting that the stock must go. The meeting was a stormy one lasting most of the night. The trustees were upset by the unusual conditions in which they were deliberating and by the unorthodox dress and manners of the students, but they listened to speaker after speaker.

Several times the chairman tried to bring the issue to a vote, but the students indicated they had more to say. Finally the chairman ruled them out of order, and for a moment it looked as though the radical elements might gain control of the crowd and physically dispossess the trustees. Moderates did prevail; the group left and a vote was taken.

Your Decision: As a member of the Board of Trustees, are you going to vote to sell the stock or to keep it?

STOP! Make your decision before proceeding.

Questions and Issues:
1. What criteria for investing money should a university follow?
2. Should such criteria include moral considerations such as investing in cigarette companies, war material companies, racist companies?

Further Involvement: Find out what guidelines your university uses in buying and selling stock and property held for investment purposes.

What Actually Happened: The Board of Trustees voted to keep the stock.

4

Racial Issues

Racial prejudice is an ancient problem, and while it is not unique to the campus scene, events during the last fifteen years have created a climate on our nation's campuses that is unique in the history of higher education. Each of the following cases was chosen to illustrate decisions which must be made on college campuses involving racial prejudice.

During the middle 1950s, society became increasingly sensitive to the fact that blacks did not have an equal opportunity with whites to achieve similar goals. Many college students seized this issue as a means of expressing idealism. Many became involved emotionally and physically in the civil rights marches and sit-ins that were characteristic of the '50s. Universities, too, became more sensitive—sensitive to the fact that they may have contributed to the problem of unequal opportunity for blacks. They began to examine the racial structure of their student bodies and discovered that very few black students were enrolled.

Faculties became aware of the injustices and supported decisions to recruit blacks who could not otherwise afford to come. Staff were hired to organize programs, provide tutoring, obtain financial aid, and so forth, in an effort to increase the number of successful black graduates, but these efforts have not been sufficient to prevent problems from arising.

FIRE HIM!

Decision Problem: The Concerned Black Students Committee is demanding that Mr. Brown be removed as head of Project Phoenix. Prior to his work with the Project, Mr. Brown was very active in civil rights work. He helped in Mississippi during Martin Luther King's confrontations, he fought for equal housing legislation, and he helped organize the black-white protest against Dain Company that resulted in a change of company employment policies. Several nonwhites are now working for Dain.

36

After his Dain success, Mr. Brown obtained a grant from a private foundation and enough federal money to implement Project Phoenix, a program in which fifty black students from urban core areas could enroll in the university each year. Students in the project are not normally admissible under regular academic standards, are from deprived homes, and require financial assistance. Project funds provide for housing, tutoring, counseling, and tuition.

Project Phoenix has progressed rapidly because Mr. Brown has been successful in overcoming red tape and resistance on the part of certain university officials. The general consensus is that without his initial efforts and tireless search for resources, Project Phoenix would not be as successful as it is.

Yet, the Concerned Black Students Committee is not asking but is demanding that Mr. Brown be fired. The Committee supports its demand by stating that Mr. Brown is not black. All else is irrelevant, they say. Disadvantaged blacks need a black administrator who understands them as no white can. No compromise is possible.

Your Decision: You are the president of the university and the Concerned Black Students Committee asks you to remove Mr. Brown within a reasonable length of time. The Committee also gives a written statement to the campus newspaper which publishes the demand. How are you going to respond? What action are you going to take?

STOP! Make your decision before proceeding.

Questions and Issues:
1. Under what conditions should student groups be able to choose their own administrator?
2. When university policy is against discrimination by reason of race or color, can one justify giving admission preference to black persons and still be consistent with the policy?
3. What are the side effects of agreeing to a demand that would not have been granted if it had merely been requested through proper channels?
4. What does the general public reaction against "giving in to students" have to do with this kind of decision?

Further Involvement:
1. Write a paper about what justice and opportunity in terms of higher education really mean for blacks. Comment on how implementation of your ideas should take place.

38

2. Role-play a situation in which the decision-maker talks the matter over with Mr. Brown.
3. Determine what your university is doing to increase the number of successful black graduates. Do you approve of what is being done?
4. Try to determine the number of blacks on your campus. Try to determine the number of nonblack, nonwhites on your campus.

What Actually Happened: Mr. Brown was moved laterally within the university to the position of special projects coordinator and was appointed to a committee studying structure and administration of all programs involving black students. At this time Project Phoenix was the only operating program, but several others were being planned, and the president directed the committee to advise him on coordinating the various programs and avoiding future problems. The president also asked the committee for advice concerning the selection of a black replacement for Mr. Brown. In addition to Mr. Brown, a white student affairs dean, an interested white faculty member, and two black faculty members were appointed to the committee. Four black students were also added as nonvoting committee members.

BLACK VERSUS NEGRO

In recent years, institutions of higher learning have discovered that there are very few members of minority groups on their faculty and administrative staffs. Almost any black person could have told them this, but white institutions had not bothered to be concerned until the 1960s. When universities started looking for qualified blacks, they found the number limited and the competition intense. They also discovered that some of the blacks who could work best with whites were not accepted by other blacks. The latter militantly accused the former of being "Uncle Tom traitors."

This dichotomy of disadvantaged black rejecting successful black has resulted in the peculiar semantic entanglement of a black-skinned Negro being "white" and has added an unfathomable dimension to the black-white problem. One black recently told me in reference to the Project Phoenix case, "The coordinator must be a Black. Only a Black can fully understand the experience of the Black man in America. He must not be a Negro." When asked for a clarification of the term *Negro,* he responded, "A Negro is one who tolerates the racist oppressions coming down on his own people and on himself."

A Decision Problem: Suppose you are a white departmental chairman who has hired a black professor for your department and now most of the black students are rejecting him as a Negro and are demanding that you hire a black faculty member.

Your Decision: What are you going to do?

A Decision Problem: Now suppose you are a dean who has hired a black assistant to advise you and to coordinate exchange programs with Black colleges in the South, only to be told by a group of Black students that you need other advice because your assistant does not speak for the Black students at all.

Your Decision: What are you going to do?

A Decision Problem: Assume you are the Negro in these two examples. You have succeeded by your own impetus. You worked your way through college and into a good position. You want to help members of your own race, but you are convinced that help must come through cooperation and integration rather than by unilateral demands and separatism. You know the Black militants want a Black hired to replace you.

Your Decision: What are you going to do?

STOP! Make your decisions before proceeding.

Questions and Issues:
1. Is Black prejudice against Negroes and whites the same kind of preconceived judgment as the traditional white against black prejudice?
2. What are the treatments or solutions for prejudice?

Further Involvement: If you are white, talk with some militant Blacks about their feelings toward Negroes and toward whites. Plan a group meeting of members of different races to try to "work through" hostilities directed toward each other.

DISMISSED INSTRUCTOR

Foreword: Often faculties are quite unsophisticated in the ways of minority groups and allow themselves to become enmeshed in problems they do not understand. In the case of the Dismissed Instructor, a university president had been confronted by

Blacks who wanted him to hire a particular Black instructor for the newly created Afro-American Studies Department. The Blacks were supported by an element of the faculty who thought the university owed this concession to the Blacks because of past injustices and who also thought this action would fulfill the Blacks' demands as well as end the threat of violence inherent in the situation.

The president, acting on the recommendation of the Blacks and their faculty supporters, hired the man. Sixteen weeks later the university governing body told the president to inform the man that his one-year contract would not be renewed. In this case history you are the university president.

Decision Problem: Committees of black students, white students, black and white students, and faculty are protesting your dismissal of Mr. Stewart, an instructor in the new Afro-American Studies Department. You have told Mr. Stewart his one-year contract will not be renewed because he is advocating physical violence against university administrators and is telling black students to come to campus armed in order to secure their "rights" more quickly. He spends his classroom time teaching black power and organizing black student disruptions.

The current protest is resulting in classroom disruptions, open confrontations between white professors and students boycotting classes, and hit-and-run damage in the library and dormitories. Few students are able to attend classes. Community feeling is running high against the college for allowing this state of near anarchy to exist. No sign of reduced protest activity is evident.

Your Decision: What are you going to do?

STOP! Make your decision before proceeding.

Questions and Issues:
1. What is academic freedom? Does it give Mr. Stewart the right to teach what he feels should be taught?
2. How can it be used to attack the president's dismissal action?

Further Involvement: Role-play Mr. Stewart and the president as they confront each other.

What Actually Happened: The president attempted to convince the protesters and their supporters that Mr. Stewart's continued presence on the faculty would lead to greater confrontations and future violence. Some dissidents were convinced, but a hard core of students and faculty continued to feel that Mr. Stewart should be rehired if that was what the Blacks wanted. The president refused to rehire Mr. Stewart, and protests continued until he finally called in city police. Several students were arrested but the opposition continued, and parts of the campus were in turmoil the rest of the year. The president did keep all classrooms open, and most of the college continued to function normally.

FORSAKEN BY PARENTS AND FRIENDS

As the number of black students on campuses increases, as interest in black students increases, it is perhaps natural that racially mixed couples are more commonplace. In some circles, it is the thing to do for white girls to be seen with black boys. The campus community has accepted mixed couples generally but many people have not, and this has placed involved students in a difficult situation.

Foreword: In this little drama you are Kathy, a university sophomore who took her black boyfriend home to meet her parents. Her parents were upset, and her father tried to persuade her to quit dating the boy. She refused and they drove back to the university the next morning.

Immediately Kathy's father began checking on the boy and discovered he had been in trouble with the university and with city police three times. The most recent city charge was disorderly conduct following a raid on the boy's apartment the last week of school. Kathy had been questioned by the police about the boy's activities.

When Kathy returned to her apartment, her roommates told her she would have to move. They said she was causing too much trouble; they did not trust her boyfriend and did not want him in their apartment. Kathy accused them of being racists and, furious, returned to her home for the second time, only until she could find another apartment. Her father met her with an ultimatum: either quit going with her boyfriend or stay away from home. She turned around and drove back to the apartment.

Decision Problem: You, Kathy, sit and stare around the empty room. Maybe now you can begin to think, with your roommates gone. It's almost a week since they told you to move because of the trouble you were causing them.

You're scared. You know someone is following you. Is it the police or could it possibly be someone hired by your parents, or maybe someone else, maybe from the office of student affairs. Just before school ended the police broke up a party at your boyfriend's apartment because of a neighbor's complaint. They're out to get him. You know that. Probably because he's black. Why can't your folks understand you have no intention of marrying him?

You can't get help from home. How can you pay your tuition next semester? Where can you live? Who are these people following you? What should you do? You feel you just have to talk to somebody before you "go to pieces." But who? Counselors are paid by student affairs. Could you really trust one?

Your Decision:

You've got to do something right now, but what?

STOP! Make your decision before proceeding.

Questions and Issues:

1. If you were a professor and Kathy came to you, what would you tell her?
2. Given unlimited resources, what kind of help would you provide for Kathy? What do you see as the purpose of such help? Be specific.
3. What is the solution to the problem of helping students who might benefit from counseling but who won't contact a counselor?
4. If you had a very sensitive matter (your roommate is distributing "pot") you wished to discuss with someone, would you contact a counselor? If not, why?
5. Would it help if someone from the university talked with her father?

Further Involvement:

1. Student affairs office is in an ambiguous position in the minds of many students. It traditionally has been the disciplinary arm of the university, and yet it provides services that have nothing to do with discipline and are oriented toward helping the student. Suggest an organizational pattern that might eliminate this duality. Do you think the university wants to retain this duality for its own purposes?
2. Suggest an informational campaign that a counseling center might use to reverse a negative image in the minds of students.

3. Describe a counseling center as you think it ought to be. Show your description to ten students and have them indicate what kinds of problems they would take to your center.

**What
Actually
Happened:**

Kathy became so upset and so in need of someone to talk to she went to Professor Nee. She did not know him, but she was desperate, and she remembered one of her girlfriends had remarked that he was one person you could really talk to.

Professor Nee was neither a psychologist nor a counselor, but noting her emotional condition, he agreed to talk to her. She rambled on for an hour and a half. He let her do most of the talking, only occasionally asking questions, expressing concern, or pointing out things he thought were appropriate. When she had run out of verbal steam, he had no solutions to offer. All of the regular offices at the university were closed, and he didn't know if anyone could help her. She said she could stay with a friend over the weekend and that she would not do anything "rash."

He did suggest she go to the counseling center, to a minister, a doctor, or an assistant dean in the student affairs on Monday morning for professional assistance. She said she thought that might be a good idea. The professor asked her to come back after she had done so. She agreed, and after thanking him for his interest and time, left his office.

Professor Nee thought about her most of the weekend and wondered what else he could do to help. She did not come back to see him, and as far as he could determine, she did not visit any of the suggested persons. She did stay in school, but he did not know where she was living or how things worked out for her. He never saw her again.

5

Student Power

Student activists, like poets, have a universal language, sometimes of love and sometimes of war and sometimes of the establishment, and very often of student power. If you ask a student activist at any university, "Who runs the University?" he will snap into a monologue that can be repeated almost verbatim on campuses throughout the world. Lynn Heinzerling interviewed student activists in Europe for an Associated Press article in April, 1969. The next three quotes are from his article.

From Rome University: "We want university reforms and a 'new society.' We object to an education geared to provide the technicians for a technological age."

Daniel Cohn-Bendit who sparked rebellions in 1968 at the Sorbonne wrote, "The university has in fact become a sausage machine which turns out people without any real culture and incapable of thinking for themselves, but trained to fit into the economic system of a highly industrialized society."

Jean Daniel Benard, vice-president of the National Union of French Students, wrote, "Society and the university are linked together, and our goals for the university cannot be brought about under the present society."

Also during the spring of 1969, Berkeley, California, radicals printed a thirteen-point 'Manifesto' in the underground newspaper, *Barb,* to spell out the hopes and dreams of the radical student revolution. Four of the thirteen points are included here: (3) . . . "The basic issue is creating an educational system in which students have real power and which prepares the young to participate in a revolutionary world." (4) "We will destroy the university unless it serves the people . . . students should not recognize the false authority of the regents." (10) "We will defend ourselves against law and order. . . . We shall abolish the tyrannical police forces not chosen by the people." (12) "We will create a people's government. We propose a referen-

44

dum to dissolve the present government, replacing it with one based on the tradition of direct participation of the people."

At Harvard University in April, 1969, students nailed up posters proclaiming *The Strikers' Manifesto.* "Strike for the eight demands. Strike because you hate cops. Strike because your roommate was clubbed. Strike to stop expansion. Strike to seize control of your life. Strike to become more human. Strike to return Paine Hall scholarships. Strike because there's no poetry in your lectures. Strike because classes are a bore. Strike for power. Strike to smash the Corporation. Strike to make yourself free. Strike to abolish ROTC. Strike because they are trying to squeeze the life out of you. Strike."

The purpose of this chapter is to examine student power and its effects on decision-makers in higher education. Confrontations demand decisions. Even "nonnegotiable demands" require responses, and decisions and responses are more credible if they are based on fact. What are some facts about student power and university government?

One interesting fact is that student demands for participation in university government is not peculiar to the 1960s. In medieval universities, students had nearly supreme power in the government of their colleges. They paid professors and so could hire and fire instructors at will. They enjoyed freedom from taxation and military service and often were free from arrest and trial in civil courts. It was not until the beginning of the sixteenth century that the concept of *in loco parentis* was beginning to be recognized at Oxford and Cambridge. Since these institutions were used as models in establishing colleges in the American colonies during the seventeenth and eighteenth centuries, and since the Puritan ethnic was dominant at that time, the idea of faculty control remained and developed with the American university system until very recently (Cardozier, 1968).

Following World War II, older veterans returning to campus obviously were beyond the point of living in dormitories or abiding by strict social rules. About the same time, seventeen- and eighteen-year-olds who had been raised during the era of more liberalized home atmospheres were entering college. These two types of "new breed" students began to demand more voice in managing their nonacademic lives while attending the university.

More and more universities added students to housing committees and social life committees, and student associations were represented on numerable committees dealing with academic affairs. By the time student activists instigated strikes and violence on campuses throughout the country, many universities had already been listening to student criticisms and were trying to remedy as many as feasible. The unwieldy structure for change on complex campuses, added to the desire for more power by students exuberant over early successes, has resulted in the daily demands by radical activists to plan the curriculum, hire and fire faculty, and regulate actions taken by governing bodies. About the only demand not made by some segment of the student body is the honor of paying for the university.

An interesting fact concerning the student charge of the "unfeeling, depersonalized university" is that the flagrant student demands have come on small, supposedly personal, campuses as well as large. The president of Swarthmore, a small college, died of a heart attack during student strife. Nor does it seem to make any difference if college administrations have included students in decision-making processes. Oberlin University in Ohio was disrupted by students who ignored their own faculty-student committees. San Francisco State, Cornell, and Harvard have had student-oriented administrations for years. Columbia suffered its worst disturbances, not before, but after it had made great progress toward reform.

In one way or another, the student power issue relates to all issues of academic policy and ultimately of academic freedom, both faculty and student. In some cases the power issue is self-evident; in many others it is hidden. Examples of it may be found in the Perilous Job Interview Decision, Trustee's Conflict of Interest, Fire Him, and the Dismissed Instructor. Whether hidden or evident, student power creates problems that students and faculty must face every day.

A nonviolent but obvious attempt to wield power is the case of the committee of three white faculty, two black faculty, and two black students which was appointed to recommend curriculum for a black studies department. The two students refused to serve unless more students were appointed; the black faculty members supported them. Ultimately more students were added as nonvoting members. A more forceful attempt to secure student control of fundamental decision processes is illustrated in the following nonnegotiable demands case.

THE BLACK STUDIES DEMAND

Decision Problem: You, a campus administrator, are in your office facing a group of black students. The spokesman for the group hands you three mimeographed sheets listing ten demands that, according to them, are not negotiable, and says, "We've thought about these demands carefully and have decided there's no basis for compromise. Either simple justice prevails and you meet our demands or we'll go on strike."

You question him briefly about the demands and about their effects on the total campus. He answers by saying, "If the university really isn't a racist tool, it will proceed promptly toward meeting these demands. I have the support of all black students on campus, the student association, many faculty, and the teaching assistants association, and I know thousands of students are sympathetic to the spirit of the demands. I can shut this university down if you don't meet our demands!"

Before you have a chance to answer, the spokesman motions to the group and they leave your office. You begin reading the "10 nonnegotiable demands."

Making the Decision:

You know you cannot begin instant departments be they white studies, black studies, or green studies. You fully understand the problems of funding, of scheduling classes, of obtaining competent faculty, of designing curricula, of defining relationships between the new department and existing departments and programs, and of establishing administration mechanisms. You know it takes a minimum of one year to implement such a program on your campus. You also realize that no one on this campus, not even the president, has the authority to initiate the program nor even unilaterally agree to the demands.

You could, of course, promise the group that you will present their demands immediately to the proper people and that you are confident such a program will be initiated as soon as possible. But then, when action is not fast enough to suit the students, you will be labeled a liar, a member of a system which is full of high ideals, glib promises, and no faith!

Your Decision:

What are you going to do and say?

STOP! Make your decision before proceeding.

Questions and Issues:

1. Discuss issues involved in "crash programs" designed to correct social weaknesses inherent in a society. How can universities best serve to alleviate social injustices?
2. Discuss the relationship between academic freedom and "nonnegotiable" demands.

Further Involvement:

In some respects this case is an example of a very simple power issue. The student group is saying, "We want to make an obvious demonstration of power. We want to show that we can make the university do what we want it to do." Beyond this simplistic stand is the complex truth of university organization. Find out how programs or departments for new studies are initiated, implemented, and staffed on your campus.

The decision-maker's responses in similar situations in the past had been misquoted, so he decided to inform the spokesman that he would respond tomorrow with a written answer to be printed in the campus newspaper and to be read, by him, over the TV station.

He prepared a statement documenting in detail programs already initiated by the university for black students as well as proposed projects and a tentative timetable for implementation of each. In the statement, the university recognized the injustices dealt to minority groups and stated what it was doing to help correct the situation. The statement then listed each of the ten demands followed by an answer and an explanation of the answer. Some answers were necessarily negative. The university was not prepared to accept student hiring and firing of faculty, and student ownership of any building was prohibited by law.

The black group promptly responded that the university position was unacceptable, and unless all ten demands were met, a general strike would be instigated. The administrator answered that he could not go beyond his statement of position without the approval of the faculties involved in implementing the department. A strike was called, several hundred students demonstrated, a few students were arrested for obstructing a building entrance, and the university became yet one more item of interest in newspaper accounts of 1969 campus demonstrations.

ASSISTANTS UNITE!

Students have used a variety of methods to exert influence and to obtain power. The more rational students view violence as inviting an undesirable backlash and as being incompatible with the pursuit of a liberal education. These students have turned to the history of labor movements and have borrowed the strike as an efficient method of getting what they want. Such 1930 slogans as "Workers unite against capitalist exploiters" have been modified to "Students unite against repressive administrators."

The success of the union movement is used to justify the present student movement, and union literature has been carefully studied by student leaders. An example of one strike was given in the *Black Studies Demand* case. Another example, closer to the labor movement, follows.

A teaching assistant is sometimes a teacher, sometimes a student. He has no tenure, no job protection, and yet he performs very real and very necessary tasks. He can be over-worked with little recourse. He is in a difficult position to question his employer's labor practices since his employer may also be the one who can veto his dissertation proposal and effectively keep him from attaining a degree. It is understandable that on occasion he feels as exploited as did the workers in large industrial plants during preunion days.

It also seems understandable that when enough teaching assistants feel threatened long enough, they will join forces and organize for mutual advancement. In this case, a state legislature had proposed to reduce funds for teaching assistant salaries partially to save money and partially as a warning to the university to curb campus disorders in the future. Immediately the teaching assistants met and passed a resolution stating they would not teach if funds were reduced, and to prove they were powerful enough to use this tactic, they agreed to a three-day walkout while the legislature was deliberating.

Several irate legislators requested that faculty members identify assistants who walked out so they could be fined or dismissed. At this action, many moderate nonstriking assistants felt the legislature was using coercion to force them into line and was using them as a punitive example to the rest of the university. Many of the moderates shifted sympathies to their striking brothers.

Your Decision: The legislature is threatening to reduce available funds for teaching assistants' salaries and is calling on faculty and administration to discipline striking teaching assistants.

As a faculty member, under what conditions would you identify any of the assistants who struck?

As an administrator, what action would you take against teaching assistants who "struck" and then phoned in sick for the next five days?

STOP! Make your decisions before proceeding.

Questions and Issues: What rights and responsibilities should teaching assistants have?

Further Involvement: Determine conditions of employment of teaching assistants on your campus.

What Actually Happened: The university assured the teaching assistants that their services would be retained for the rest of the year and that none would be released. Most of the teaching assistants resumed their teaching, and the campus slowly returned to normalcy. Very few, if any, were publicly identified and disciplined in any way. The teaching assistants began efforts to form a union.

THE IMPRISONED DEPARTMENT CHAIRMAN

While some student activists demonstrate against central administration, others think they will have greater success if they deal with smaller units within the university, such as the department. One recent skirmish began when a young professor, very popular with his students, was not given tenure by his department. His dismissal became a rallying point for students who hoped to reverse this decision.

Decision Problem: Assume for the moment that the action has started. Pickets wander through the building carrying signs demanding that the young professor be rehired. For several days sporadic disruptions have occurred in classrooms, and faculty members have received phone calls at all hours of the day and night. Finally, today, the students have tried a drastic experiment to force the department to capitulate to their demand. They have succeeded in locking you, the department chairman, in your office, and they have told you that they have no intention of letting you out until you agree to call a departmental faculty meeting to reconsider the dismissal action.

Your Decision: There you are in your office. What are you going to do? There is no great rush in making your decision because you will have several hours alone behind barricaded doors in which to think.

STOP! Make your decision before proceeding.

Questions and Issues:
1. How can departmental chairmen stop student interference with departmental business?
2. Should student opinions be sought in hiring or firing faculty members?

What Actually Happened: Security guards, while on a routine building check, heard the noise and released him about an hour after he was detained. He did call a special meeting at which the case was discussed, but the department upheld its position not to give tenure to the faculty member in question.

THE HARASSED PROFESSOR

After the departmental level, the next natural area for students to exert pressure is on the individual faculty member whom they classify as irrelevant, unfair, or guilty of poor teaching. Suppose you are a professor designated by student activists as irrelevant and that during your first class, fall semester, about a dozen students begin a systematic disruption of your lectures. You give them time to state their disenchantment with the grading system, with the organization of the class, with the lack of relevant issues to be discussed, even with the immorality of the war in Vietnam, although this is irrelevant to your class.

Decision Problem: As you meet your class for the second and third sessions, you realize the hecklers are there to stay and that they are making it impossible to conduct your class as you wish. You have about 200 students in your class, and since you won't have the class roster for another week, you have no idea who the disrupters are. At the end of the third session, you hear mutterings from another dozen or so students who are tired of the disruptions and are threatening to do "something" to the hecklers. If any teaching is to be done, the classroom interruptions must be stopped. As the professor, what are you going to do about the situation?

Making the Decision: First you discuss the problem with your professional colleagues, only to discover that each one offers you different advice. You retire to your office to think.

Your Decision: What are you going to do?

STOP! Make your decision before proceeding.

Questions and Issues: What is the relationship between order in the classroom and learning?

Further Involvement: Role-play a heckling classroom situation. Have various persons play the role of the professor.

A Related Decision Problem: When you questioned your colleague who teaches history of the Civil War Period, you discovered that he has a problem of his own. During each of his class sessions since fall term began, three or four black students have taken seats at the far end of the room and have taken notes on every word he has said. They are not registered in his course, and they have not created any disturbance; they simply are recording what he says, and this makes him nervous.

One of his history students tells him he thinks they are members of the Black Militants collecting information about racist attitudes of faculty members. Your colleague asks you what he should do about their presence in his class. What advice do you give him?

**Your
Decision:**

If you were he, what would you do?

STOP! Make your decision before proceeding.

**Questions
and Issues:**

1. Should students be allowed in classes for which they have not registered?
2. Would your advice to your colleague be different if the students in question were white SDS members rumored to be collecting information about inappropriate course material and incompetent teaching?

Part Two

Timeless Troublesome Decisions

6

The Continuing Scene

The highly publicized crises on college campuses, discussed in Part One, are of recent origin and are not an inherent part of the university system. The fundamental goal of a university is to provide a higher education for those who can profitably pursue it, and dialogue about racial issues, student power, morality is but one aspect of this goal. Universities have had, and will continue to have, problems that relate to the fundamental goal. These problems provide the subject matter for the second part of this book.

Back in the days when ten percent of the population attended college, these continuing problems were ignored by most people as being of interest only to a few absent-minded professors. Now when about eighty percent of all high school seniors talk about going to college, problems of higher education affect a large number of people.

A college education has become very important in our society as the road to marriage, higher status, better jobs, and better living conditions. There is considerable pressure on colleges to admit as many students as possible and to fulfill the expectations of all these diverse creatures. While education is as important to as many as it is today and while rules regulating the educational system are as inadequate, complicated, and dissatisfying to as many as they are today, problems will continue. The two narratives that follow illustrate this point.

SALLY TURNER—CO-ED

Sally Turner has problems. Most of the time she handles her troubles pretty well, but some days are impossible—like this morning. Her roommate woke her up again. Sally's a night person. She gets a lot of hard, productive studying done at night, but in the morning she's out of it and wants to sleep. Her roommate is an early riser and makes enough noise to waken the whole dorm; and this morning, again, she woke Sally up. They had a spat, and Sally started for her first class in a grumpy mood. She'd had it. Right after lunch she was going over to the housing office and ask for a different room.

Right now here she was, half way across campus heading for a stupid class that had been a bore all semester. The professor used the same lecture notes he'd used twenty-five years ago, and the textbook was so old its only value was as an antique. If she got there early enough, she could get a back seat and catch up on her sleep. But there was no class that morning. When Sally reached the classroom, she was greeted with a closed door and a notice stating that the professor was out of the city attending a meeting. The class would meet at its regular time next week. Now Sally was really irritated. How could a professor just take off like that? Who was paying him anyway? Her dad had paid for an education, not an empty classroom.

Sally looked at her watch—9:40. She decided to go to the library and read until 10:30 when she was supposed to meet her boyfriend, Dick, at the Union. She didn't want to see him this morning either. They used to have so much fun together, but everything was changed now. When she met Dick last year she had really been impressed. He was a great guy and good looking, too. He was smarter than anyone she had ever dated, and they used to have tremendous conversations and see good movies and plays. Not this year. Last fall he had joined the Young Socialist Activist Group, and all he did now was talk, think, and do the political-line action of the group. He was after her to join, and every date turned into an argument.

Sally sat down at a library table and opened up her philosophy folder. She would have to push to get that paper in by next Friday. She'd had the assignment since the beginning of the semester but hadn't done anything on it. She'd tried once but two of the reference books were out of the library, so she hadn't gotten started. It was all busy work, anyway, she thought. What good would it ever do her to compare the historical development of two nineteenth-century philosophers? Well, one thing it would do for her, it would give her a passing grade! Like it or not, her weekend was now shot; she'd be comparing the historical development of two nineteenth-century philosophers! She began to check out references, and as she thumbed through the card catalogue, she decided to give Dick another try. He loved philosophy, and last year he would have helped her with a paper like this. Maybe, if she mentioned it just right, he'd forget his social action and give her a hand.

She was beginning to wake up now and life didn't look so gloomy. She left the library and started for the Union. As she waited in line for her cup of coffee, Marge came over to chat. Marge was in her econ class and was forever calling Sally for help with family problems. Marge's folks were after her every day to do better in school, and Marge really showed the pressure. Too bad she had to depend on her dad for money, otherwise she could take off and do what she wanted to do. Marge told Sally once that she never wanted to go to college. She wanted to stay in her home town and marry her high school boyfriend. Sally didn't know why anyone would want to do a boring thing like that, but if that's what Marge wanted out of life, her parents should let her do it.

Sally paid for her coffee and walked over to an empty table. She was figuring out how to start the philosophy bit when she saw Dick come into the room, and she wished she had stayed in the library. He had that creepy friend with him who couldn't say anything unless he spouted off Maoisms and trite phrases about the glorious days when the capitalist war mongers would be defeated. The two young men picked up their cups of coffee and joined Sally. Quick greetings were exchanged, and they immediately began tossing around the same old flowery phrases. Sally nodded at appropriate intervals without bothering to listen. She wondered to herself if it was all worth it. Maybe Marge's idea of settling down at home wasn't so bad after all.

Sally finished her coffee. Maybe she should transfer next year, or maybe she should take a semester off to think things through. She didn't have much of an interest in her major. She could switch into something like elementary teaching and then she could always get a job. But she didn't really like teaching either. Suddenly Dick waved his hand in front of her face. He was talking to her but she hadn't heard a word he was saying. He wanted to get together again that evening and listen to his new record of the Fifth Dimension. Sally thought of that stupid philosophy paper. She picked up her books, pushed her chair away from the table, and got up. As she left, she told Dick to call her about suppertime.

DEAN MUSGROVE

Dean Musgrove wheeled away from the window and expertly spun his heavy chair to the exact center of the kneehole in his desk. Let other people watch the demonstrators play their game of "Run, Sheep, Run"; he had enough work to keep him busy every day of the year. He had already plowed through lines of pickets to attend two meetings that morning. One was with the Orientation Committee to discuss the freshman orientation program. Apparently the kids weren't attending scheduled events, and the committee was trying to do something about it. The other had been an unpleasant meeting about liberalizing the language requirements. It was a heated session with members of the language departments, most of whom thought language was critical to an education. He had missed another meeting called to discuss the class attendance regulation that neither faculty nor students were paying any attention to. There just wasn't enough time for everything.

On his desk were three piles of letters, file folders, and notes, neatly stacked for him by his secretary. He picked up the top letter—a mother writing to protest that the university had not accepted her son, and she wanted an explanation from the Dean. The next letter was from a student claiming that his grades were not a true reflection of his potential and that if the Dean would just give him the chance, he would prove that he could make college. Then came about fifty routine acceptance letters that needed his signature.

Dean Musgrove went through several more letters before greeting his 10:00 appointment, Coach Brown, who felt that the anatomy professor was making it especially tough on his boys just because they were athletes. As the coach left the office, he shook hands with Professor Fiedler who was coming in to talk with the Dean. The professor wanted permission to obtain entrance test scores for a sample of fifty preeducation freshman females. Dean Musgrove called the registrar and concluded it would be too difficult to get the data, so he and Professor Fiedler spent the next thirty minutes discussing other methods of obtaining comparable data.

He was past due his next appointment, so the Dean apologetically terminated the discussion and walked Professor Fiedler to the door. Professor Cloddy walked past both of them and sat in the chair next to the desk. He came to appeal the salary raise he had been given for next year. Dean Musgrove dreaded this kind of appointment. It was always so difficult to explain that, in his opinion, activities of other professors were of more value than were those of Professor Cloddy. Dean Musgrove did the best job he could, but Dr. Cloddy answered that politics was involved in his case, not merit. Musgrove was relieved when the hour was over and it was lunch time. He hurried to meet Dean Slusser who wanted to have lunch and talk about the declining enrollment in the Honors Program.

After lunch he walked to the other end of campus to attend a meeting of the Classroom Assignment Committee which was trying to find better ways to schedule classes. Professors just don't like teaching early morning, late afternoon, evening, or Saturday class sections. The problem had become a source of friction and was of much concern to the committee. When he returned to his office, his assistant was waiting to ask if the ambiguous policy about credit by examination had been clarified. Copy deadline for *The Bulletin* had been yesterday, and the credit problem was one of the items holding up the printing. The Dean called the committee chairman, who was not in his office, so he left word to have him call back when he returned. The assistant left, and Dean Musgrove called the chairman of the art department who wanted a policy statement about teaching assistants who were absent from their classroom duties. He told the chairman he did not think the university had ever formulated such a policy, but he would check into the matter and call him back as soon as possible.

He shunted these matters aside for a few minutes and began to work on a speech for an alumni Booster Dinner next month. He had been requested to give this speech, and he wanted to do a good job. He understood that the people from that area were upset with, what they called, loose morals and improper supervision of students on the campus. He also recollected that the same district had voted against the increased appropriations bill for higher education. What would be a good, positive opener for his speech? Just as some ideas began to come, his secretary announced that the director of admissions had arrived to request an exception to the newly adopted austerity measure that no secretary would be allowed overtime pay.

The director left at 5:15 and the Dean had promised his wife he would be home by 5:30, for sure, tonight. He quickly checked his calendar for tomorrow and decided he had better work on his speech at home after dinner. He'd probably better outline the rest of his letters, too, so his secretary could type them first thing in the morning. He left his office and glanced toward the Mall to see if there was any student protest activity going on.

PEOPLE AND RULES

Why do Sally, the Dean, and thousands of others in universities continue to have troubles? Mostly because of people. A university is composed of people drawn together to study, discuss, investigate, and learn, and the usual problems are present—fights for territory, status, jobs, and money. Some of the people attack each other and jealously vie for each other's attention and affection. Many try to persuade others that their way is the best or only way to solve a problem. Some are greedy and want "more"—more power, pot, freedom, travel, secretaries, time for leisure. They question the motives and capabilities of each other. Because of differences in age, attitudes, interests, and philosophy, they often cannot agree on appropriate solutions for mutual concerns.

Just as society has found it necessary to establish rules and codes of conduct to limit the behavior of individuals for the common good, so has the microsociety, called a university. Such rules and codes are not unanimously accepted. Some are imposed on others by those with authority or status; some, wrought by compromise, are not really satisfactory to anyone. Rules democratically voted in are satisfactory only to the majority while the minority resists. In almost every case, rules and codes are apt to be offensive and unsatisfactory to many people affected by them.

Some rules and codes are vague, "Students found guilty of misconduct will be punished." Some are unwritten, but generally followed, "Department chairmen do not go into classrooms to evaluate the teaching effectiveness of their faculty members." Other rules exist because of honored tradition, "The department member with longest seniority has first choice of courses and times to teach." Some codes are known only to small peer groups, "Jewish students from the East apply for dorm X and gentiles from the Midwest apply for dorm Y." Or, on a slightly different tact, "Graduate students are graded on their own curve separate from undergraduates in the same class." At least one written rule is openly flouted, "No smoking in the classroom."

People inside and outside the university community become annoyed and frustrated because these rules are not explicitly written and assembled in one place and because they are interpreted and applied in so many different ways. The resulting ambiguity creates the inevitable situation where the right hand does not know what the left is doing or where neither hand knows what it is supposed to be doing.

One large university discovered that an official policy regarding confidentiality of information was unknowingly being violated in the dean of student's office because part-time student help had unlimited access to personal files of hundreds of students.

In a complex institution, rules are necessary, but there are always people who feel that in their case an exception should be made. Four cases of such requests are presented in chapter 7.

People often need help. Chapter 8 cites four studies of people who solicited or offered help and the complications that followed. Decisions about the use of confidential information are discussed in chapter 9, and chapter 10 deals with problems unique to professional schools. How much power should faculty members have over students is the touchy subject matter for chapter 11.

7

Exceptions to the Rules

Universities establish rules specifying minimum and maximum credits that students may carry at one time and deadlines for adding or dropping credits. These rules are partially justified on the assumption that new students do not know how much academic work they can handle satisfactorily. Registration regulations also enable more students to complete courses of their choice. If there were no rules, a student might sign up for many courses, select a few, and drop the rest, leaving vacancies too late for others to enter.

Once rules are established, however, circumstances inevitably arise where enforcement of the rules appears to be unfair to a particular student. Since students are taught to think for themselves and not to blindly follow rules established by others, it is natural that universities have an inordinate number of requests for exceptions to rules. Provision for a reviewing authority is necessary. At some institutions deans consider exception requests, while at other schools faculty committees are elected or appointed for this purpose.

FACULTY ADVISORY COMMITTEE PROBLEM

Foreword: You are a member of a faculty advisory committee that regularly meets the eleventh week of each semester to consider requests for exception to the rule, "Courses may not be dropped after the end of the ninth week of class."

Decision Problem: The committee meeting is in session, and the chairman has given each member a copy of six requests to be considered and decided by them. You and your colleagues begin reading.

In essence, student number one says: "I know I'm past the deadline and I don't have any excuse. I had drop cards made out and just forgot to turn them in. I know I goofed, but if you check my record, you'll see I have good grades and have not asked for anything special before. No one is perfect. Is the University so rigid I can't get one break?"

61

Student number two writes: "I became involved in a civil rights protest and missed a week of school, which would have been no problem, but then I became ill and missed another week of classes. When I started back to school, I still felt pretty weak. I also need more money so I've started working on Saturdays." Attached to the request is a medical statement verifying a four-day illness.

Ignorance of drop rules is the plea of student number three. "I'm a transfer student," he writes, "and at my former school there were no drop rules. Why didn't somebody here tell me about them? I've had nothing but trouble since I came here. First I was misclassified at registration, then I was canceled out of a class because it was filled. I had a terrible time getting a ruling on a course I had taken before. It may or may not duplicate one I'm taking now. I still haven't been able to find out if I'll get credit for it. Moving to a big, depersonalized institution like this is difficult, and I should think a transfer student would get a little extra help."

Student number four has never dropped a course before. He did poorly in a mid-term exam just before the drop deadline, but instead of dropping the course, he viewed the low grade as a personal challenge to make a go of the class. Now he realizes he should have dropped it while he legally could. He says that he will be lucky to get a *D* even with special help, and he will lose his scholarship for next year if he doesn't maintain his present grade-point average. He claims that he cannot continue in school without financial help.

"I'm no brain, just a hard-working student who has to study hard to get passing grades," student number five writes. "I'm from a hard-working, law-abiding family who take pride in doing a good day's work. Now I'm flunking this course. I shouldn't have taken it in the first place, but I've never backed away from anything in my life just because it was difficult. I know several students who have asked to drop courses after the deadline and have been denied, and I suppose that will be my fate, too. I get the very uncomfortable feeling, however, that if I blew up family problems or illness, pleaded anxiety or depression, spun a pathetic yarn, or if I were a black, disadvantaged student from the slums of Chicago, I could probably get permission to drop."

Student number six is a second-semester black student recruited during the university's drive to help disadvantaged members of society. He is flunking one course and is in danger of flunking another one. At the end of his first semester, he was put on probation because of academic difficulties. The request has been sent to the faculty committee, not by the student, but by the professor of the class the student is flunking.

Making the Decision: Which of the six students will you let drop the unwanted course?

(yes) (no)
1.
2.
3.
4.
5.
6.

STOP! Make your decision before proceeding.

Questions and Issues:
1. (a) If you agreed to let all six drop, are you also agreeing to the proposition that any student should be allowed to change courses at any time he chooses? If not, define a rule you would be willing to enforce.
(b) If you will not let any of the six drop, cite an example of circumstances you feel warrants an exception.
(c) If you will let one or more but not all six drop, state the reasons for your action, or the critical differences between petitions.
2. Should a faculty advisory committee seek or demand independent verification of the circumstances of each student who requests an exception?
3. What would happen if universities had no rules about number of courses carried or no deadlines for adding or dropping courses?
4. How can logical rules regulating such matters be formulated?

Further Involvement:
1. Discuss the cases by role-playing the committee's deliberations.
2. Survey students and faculty at your school about their knowledge of such rules and how adequate or reasonable they think they are. Use the results of your survey to propose changes.

What Actually Happened: Decisions for problems like these depend on the philosophy of the campus and the attitudes of individual committee members. Committee members sometimes change their decisions when presented with similar cases.

The committee studying these requests decided to let number three and number six drop their courses.

GRADUATION REQUIREMENTS

Exceptions-to-the-rules problems about all kinds of college requirements occur at every academic level. Here are four examples that pertain to quality and quantity of course work required for graduation. You must make a decision in each case. The requests are for exception to the rule that students must have 120 credits and 240 grade points, *twice as many grade points as credits,* in order to graduate; that is, they must have maintained a *C* average for eight semesters, or four years, on all work completed. Simply acquiring extra grade points is not sufficient.

Decision Problem:

1. Student number one requests he be allowed to graduate with 120 credits but only 239 grade points.
2. Student number two wishes to graduate with 120 credits but only 238 grade points.
3. Student number three has 123 credits and 241 grade points.
4. Student number four has 124 credits and only 240 grade points, but he is requesting that the college drop an *F,* "0" points for a 4-credit engineering math course he took as a freshman before he switched to Spanish. (If the engineering math *F* is dropped from his record, he will meet the 120 credits and 240 grade points requirement.)

Making the Decision:

Will you decide to let the students graduate?

(yes)   (no)

1.
2.
3.
4.

STOP! Make your decision before proceeding.

Questions and Issues:

1. How might the size of a university make a difference in a decision like this?
2. Would your decision be different if you could quietly grant an exception that no other student would know about?

Further Involvement:

1. Try to draft a policy covering exclusion of courses for persons transferring majors.
2. Role-play student number 2 presenting his request in person before the faculty committee. Remember that one of the problems faced by such committee members is that students are often quite persuasive and can come across in a more logical manner than the rule itself.

Student number 2 might argue that he had taken a much tougher curriculum under professors who were generally recognized as tough graders than other students who had taken snap courses under "soft" professors. He might charge that the university is encouraging students to take easy courses by not differentiating among quality and levels of difficulty.

What Actually Happened: At large universities there may be many students with similar requests, so administrators are concerned about establishing precedents for students past (who still have not graduated), present, and future. In these cases, number four was granted a degree because engineering courses were not considered to be intrinsic to his liberal arts degree; numbers one, two, and three were not awarded degrees at that time.

ADMISSIONS DECISION

Other university rules set minimum number of credits in residence, dates for payment of fees, specific course requirements, attendance in class, and requirements for admission. Trying to defend these rules by the use of logic is often futile. How can one defend a graduation requirement of 120 credits and 240 grade points versus one of 118 credits and 235 grade points? Or is a 50 percentile admission requirement more defensible than a 45 percentile admission requirement? Decision-makers are open targets for those who seek exceptions, because there are often many more reasons for granting one exception than there are reasons for not granting it.

Foreword: The admission rule for freshmen at State University reads: "Students must be in the upper half of their high school graduating class, must have a recommendation from an official of their high school, and must have taken and received an acceptable score on one of the recognized college entrance examinations." Acceptable is currently defined as 40th percentile. You are a member of a faculty committee appointed to review special requests for admission that do not meet these minimum requirements.

Decision Problem: You and the other committee members are listening to the Director of Admissions as he explains the admission rules and then hands each of you these five special requests.

Student number one is technically not admissible. Clipped to the application is a letter written by the boy's father and originally sent to the president who had forwarded it to the admissions office with the comment added that the father is on the appropriations subcommittee of the state legislature. The father had written, "My son is no genius, but he is a good, solid citizen who participates in school and community activities and works hard. I believe the university represents the best education he can get, and as a loyal alumnus working hard for the university, I believe he deserves the chance to prove he can do it."

Student number two is technically not admissible. He is the star quarterback on a high school team in a town not far from the university. He made the all-state football team and is generally recognized as future college star material. Attached to the boy's application is an urgent, personal request for admission written by the university football coach who has not had a good team for several years. The coach has added statements from the boy's counselor, principal, and high school teachers who think he has sufficient academic potential to make it at the university.

Student number three is not eligible because he did not take a college entrance examination. He is blind and had no thought of attending college when the tests were given. Now he thinks he can succeed.

Student number four is technically not eligible because he dropped out of high school with poor grades. He has been working and has now decided he wants a college education. He took a college entrance examination and made the 75th percentile.

Request number five is a letter from parents inquiring why the university has not notified their son as to whether or not he has been accepted. The parents claim they mailed the application two months ago, but the admissions office has no record of receiving their application. If the facts given in the letter are true, the son is eligible, but the deadline for admission applications is six weeks past, and it is now too late to obtain necessary information and routinely process the application in time for registration next term.

Making the Decision:

What will your answer be to the five requests?

(yes)   (no)

1.
2.
3.
4.
5.

STOP! Make your decision before proceeding.

Should there be one admission standard or should there be several which take into account regional and state quotas, nonstate quotas, racial quotas, intended majors, quality of high school, and so forth?

What are the admission policies at your university?

Number five was notified that his application would be considered next session instead of the impending term, and the university was sorry if it erred.

Letters were sent to one, two, three, and four, explaining that their chances for success were small, and if they wished to remain under consideration, they would have to come to the university for a personal conference with the admissions officer. After the conference, one, three, and four were told they could be admitted, but three withdrew his application and four decided to take two night courses before quitting his job to become a full-time student.

INDECISION

Bonnie couldn't decide which of two courses to drop. She had come to the dean's office the first week of the semester to ask advice. The office secretary had checked the number of credits for each course and told her she could drop either since each would count as an elective; neither was required. Bonnie told her she knew this, but she simply couldn't decide which one she wanted to take, and she asked for further help.

The secretary took her in to see the assistant to the dean. He discussed with Bonnie the content of each course and what information she might hope to gain from each. He told her either one would be valuable and that he had no basis for advising her to drop one or the other, the decision should be hers.

The next day Bonnie called the office and asked to see someone other than the assistant to the dean because he would not tell her which course to drop. The secretary made an appointment with a graduate student in counseling who was taking a practicum in the office. From Bonnie's record, the student learned she was a junior and had received all A's and B's during four previous semesters. This information made him wonder why she said she needed advice and why she said she was afraid of doing poorly in one of the two courses. He asked why she didn't drop the course she was so concerned about, and she answered, "Because I liked it." He then suggested she drop the other one, but she said she was doing well in it, and she thought it might be valuable to her. He next suggested keeping them both, and she replied that both would be too heavy a schedule for her. They discussed the matter for half an hour, and when Bonnie left, the practicum student had the feeling nothing had been accomplished.

The visits and phone calls continued, and when the deadline for dropping courses arrived, everyone in the dean's office knew Bonnie's predicament and all were perplexed. They had never seen anyone so upset over such a trivial matter. On the final day before the deadline, Bonnie came in and told the secretary she still could not decide between the courses. She said she hadn't slept the night before and desperately needed advice. By now, the secretary had lost patience with her and told her there was no one else in the office she could talk to and reminded her that that was the final day for dropping courses.

Bonnie reluctantly filled out a drop card for one of the courses and left the office, obviously unhappy. That night Bonnie called the assistant to the dean at his home, told him she had filled out a drop card for one of the courses but had changed her mind and wanted to drop the other course. Could she? She paused and then asked if she couldn't have until tomorrow to decide and come in to talk the situation over again with him.

Making the Decision: You are the assistant to the dean and you are holding the phone, what are you going to tell Bonnie?

STOP! Make your decision before proceeding.

Questions and Issues:
1. This case was handled by an assistant. Do you think he should have talked it over with his superior before deciding?
2. How much time can one staff member justify spending on a problem like this?
3. Does Bonnie need further counseling? If you feel she does, how would you arrange it?

Further Involvement: Role-play a situation in which one person asks another to help him decide which courses to take but then raises objections to each helpful idea. Note the helper's emotional reactions as the situation proceeds.

What Actually Happened: The assistant to the dean knew that he should say, "It's too late to drop courses. You've had enough time and help in making this decision and there is no advantage to be gained by prolonging this affair. Your classes stand as of 5:00 P.M. this afternoon."

However, the assistant did not say this. He thought to himself that people just didn't get upset over such a routine matter and that something else must be bothering Bonnie, but no new clues were offered during the phone conversation. He refused to comment on the request to switch drop cards, but he did say he would talk with her one more time.

When he arrived at his office the next morning, Bonnie was waiting for him. She told him she had worried all night and had not slept. She acted nervous and looked like she might begin to cry momentarily. She told him she had always had trouble making up her mind but never to this extent before.

The assistant finally allowed her to switch drop cards. He told her this would be the last time she could change and that she should forget about the decision and just get to work on her courses. She thanked him and left. But as the reader might guess, Bonnie came back later.

8

Providing Relevant Help

Universities are peopled with helpers. At one time or another, nearly every person in higher education helps someone directly or indirectly. Obvious helpers, such as counselors, deliberately place themselves in a helping position where those in trouble can find them. And come they do, some with unemotional, straightforward pleas for help, others with requests well hidden by devious words and secondary problems, and still others send a stand-in to seek help for them.

One job of the helper in these cases is to determine how best to provide relevant help. Each of the four students in this chapter is distressed and is no longer able to rationally cope with a problem area in his life. Each seeks help, but each does it in a different way or for a different reason. You, the helper, will find yourself in four unique situations. Will you be able to provide the best relevant help each time?

THE GIRL WHO WAS UPSET

Foreword: People talk to themselves and to or with each other for an infinite number of reasons. Conversation is used to seek facts, make new friends, persuade, scold or punish, relieve anxiety, express happiness or unhappiness, and to ask for help. Occasionally words appear to form a simple request concerning some routine matter, but actually they are cover-ups for other kinds of problems. In chapter 7, the assistant to the dean thought Bonnie's request for more time to make a decision might have hidden meanings. As he put it, "People don't get this upset over such a trivial matter." However, he didn't pick up any significant clues during their conversations, so he handled her request as routine and moved on to other business. But Bonnie's words had other meanings, and just because the assistant couldn't identify them does not mean they were not there.

Decision Problem: You, a dean in a small university, are answering correspondence when your assistant comes in to ask advice about a very distraught girl in his office. He hands you her folder and says, "I've talked with her several times during the semester about which of the two electives to take. She signed up for both, then wanted to drop one but couldn't decide which one. She changed her mind several times, and I thought I saw the last of her two days ago when I allowed her to change again and drop one course late, but today she is back in my office pleading to drop the other one instead. I questioned the wisdom of this and she suddenly started crying. She's still sitting in there crying. Something's got to be wrong but I'm not getting anyplace with her. What do you suggest?"

You tell your assistant that you think you better see her and glancing quickly through her folder, you note her name —Bonnie, good grades, good recommendations, no evidence of previous mental health problems. The secretary comes into your office with a sobbing girl. She tries to tell you what the trouble is, mentioning adding and dropping courses, but she is still too upset to make sense. You try to engage her in general conversation about her academic schedule, but each response on her part brings new tears.

By now you are quite concerned. You know she needs help, but you are not sure you are the one to provide it. The two of you sit quietly for about five minutes while she gets some control of herself and you try to think yourself to the real problem. Just as you are ready to suggest help from another source, Bonnie begins talking.

"I guess it really doesn't matter which course I drop. I don't care anymore. At the beginning of the semester I cared because I'd just been accepted into the nursing program for next fall, and that's what I've always really wanted to do. Now I can't anyway. I'm sure I'm pregnant, and my boyfriend says the baby can't possibly be his so he won't have anything to do with me, and I can't, I just can't tell my mother. She wouldn't do anything for me. She'd tell me not to come home."

Bonnie quits talking and looks like she's going to cry again. You quickly digest this new bit of information and then ask her if she has seen a doctor and when the baby is due. She tells you she has not seen a doctor, and that's another problem. She can't continue with a university doctor after she quits school, and she can't possibly face going to her family doctor at home. That's out! She thinks maybe the baby will be born late October or early November.

"I don't know where to go or what to do. I can stay in school the rest of this semester, but I don't know what I'll do this summer or next fall. When my father died, he left me a trust fund, administered by the bank, that pays my tuition, room, and board while I'm in college, but that stops if I leave school. I just don't know what to do."

Your Decision: Bonnie begins to cry again. What are you going to say to her? How can you really help her?

STOP! Make your decision before proceeding.

Questions and Issues:
1. What is the best way to handle people who are crying? If a person seems to be on the verge of tears, should you change the subject to avoid the crying, excuse yourself and leave the room, or hand the person a Kleenex?
2. Do you feel that Bonnie could profit from counseling? If so, in what way? If you were the dean, how would you arrange a referral?
3. How much should the dean or some other university professional do for her and how much do you feel she should do for herself, such as arranging medical help, learning about homes for unwed mothers, finding out what financial assistance might be available?

Further Involvement:
1. Role-play Bonnie's dialogue with the dean.
2. Find out what sources of help are available for a person like Bonnie in your community and find out what other professional personnel might advise in her case.

What Actually Happened: After considerable prodding, the dean persuaded Bonnie to see a doctor he recommended and if she really was pregnant, to tell her mother. Next, he encouraged her to visit a local welfare agency to find out about arrangements for unwed mothers, and finally, he asked her to talk to her boyfriend one more time. He also told her to come in and see him every other day as long as she stayed on campus to tell him how things were going.

Bonnie did see the doctor who confirmed her suspicions, and she did tell her mother who reacted as she thought she would, condemning Bonnie and telling her she couldn't possibly come home. For about three weeks after this, Bonnie's emotional state deteriorated further, but she did come to see the dean regularly, she stayed in school, and she contacted the welfare agency. She tried to talk with her boyfriend, but he continued to refuse to talk with her or see her, and she refused to press paternity charges.

She had made arrangements to stay with a friend during the summer when her mother called and apologized and told her to come home and stay until the baby was born. Bonnie did go home. She gave the baby up for adoption, and the next semester she was able to return to campus and enter the school of nursing.

THREATENING PHONE CALLS

Very few students go directly to psychiatrists, counselors, student affairs persons, or professors for help with personal problems. If they talk about them to anyone, it is apt to be to friends. A student may not be getting the professional help he needs simply because he doesn't ask for it. If a university staff member senses a student is in trouble, is it appropriate for him to intervene in any way? This possibility occurs regularly in classroom situations where professors are sensitive to the behavior of their students.

If you were a professor, what would you do about a girl who comes to class regularly and sits muttering to herself, never taking a note? Or what would you do if you ask your class if anyone knows anything about a girl who is absent every day, and her roommate tells you privately after class that the girl does nothing but eat, sleep, and sit in her room staring out the window? When or if to intervene is a perennial and difficult question to answer and, typically, there are ambiguities.

Foreword: You are dean of student affairs. An instructor has called, asking you to check on a student who he thinks needs help.

Decision Problem: The instructor hadn't questioned Joan's absence from his first Friday quiz. On Monday she had told him she'd been sick, and since he didn't give make-up tests for the weekly quiz, the incident was closed. But when the same pattern repeated itself for three consecutive weeks, the instructor became concerned and asked Joan to see him in his office.

She again told him she had been sick, but after more discussion, admitted she often became afraid and sick before exams. She said that because of this fear, general nervousness, and other personal problems, she had dropped out of school the preceding semester. She had seen a psychiatrist once at that time but had not been helped and had no plans to see him again.

Joan was sure to flunk the course if she continued to miss quizzes. When Joan left his office, the instructor called the dean of student affairs who promised to look into the situation. The next day the dean asked an assistant to call Joan and ask if she could help her. The assistant called Joan's rooming house, but when she asked for Joan, the person on the other phone hung up. Two hours later she tried again and talked with the housemother who said she would have Joan call back.

Joan did not call the assistant back, but the next day she went to the instructor's office before class. She was upset, crying, and almost incoherent. About all she could say was that she knew the administration was out to get her because she had been getting strange phone calls, and she identified some of them as coming from the student affairs office. A friend came to take Joan home, and the instructor promptly called the dean. As the dean, what will be your next move?

Making the Decision: You have no way of knowing the girl's exact problem. You are not sure what you can do to help her or even if she wants or needs help. You do not know how to explain to her why you are contacting her. Typically at your college, student personnel services are offered on a voluntary basis. Joan has not requested any assistance. Your role in this situation is ambiguous.

These were the conditions at the time you first decided to ask your assistant to call Joan. Your plan was for the assistant to identify herself and simply make her services available. Since that approach had been unsuccessful, to say the least, you must make a new decision. Consider the following alternatives.

1. Telephone Joan to offer your help.
2. Do nothing.
3. Ask the housemother in the residence to check on the situation.
4. Send the assistant to personally talk with Joan.
5. Go yourself to talk with Joan.
6. Write her a letter.
7. Contact her parents.
8. Other

Your Decision: What are you going to do?

STOP! Make your decision before proceeding.

Questions and Issues: 1. Should the university seek out and try to help students who have not asked for help but who appear to be in danger of losing their good standing in the academic community? Examples of such students are those who are failing classes and those who are not attending classes.

2. Should the university seek out and try to help students who have not asked for help but who appear to have emotional problems?

3. Relative to (1) and (2), who should do the identifying? Who should do the seeking? How should contact be made? What kinds of help are appropriate?

Further Involvement: Ask administrators in your college how they would handle situations mentioned in the above questions.

What Actually Happened: The dean sent his assistant back to talk with the housemother first and then have her send in Joan. The housemother explained to Joan that the assistant was there to help her if she wanted help. After reassuring Joan, the housemother left them alone. The assistant told Joan she had been calling her, not to check up on her or to scold her, but to see if she could help her.

They talked for almost an hour, and the assistant learned that Joan had boyfriend problems, parental health problems, and lately had developed symptoms associated with intense anxiety. She had repeatedly missed school recently and had not been able to keep up with her studies.

Now the assistant had a further decision to make, whether a doctor or a psychiatrist should be consulted. Joan was not receptive to the idea of seeing either. She thought she should drop school and work a semester before returning. The assistant was still concerned and returned the next day to help Joan get her affairs in order before she left campus. Joan promised to see her family doctor when she got home. The assistant notified appropriate parties on campus that Joan had withdrawn and the case was closed.

TRUTH MAY HURT

In the two preceding cases, the helper became involved indirectly. In this case, the helper has been deliberately sought out and must decide whether or not to help the student in a way that might be viewed by others as unethical or inappropriate.

Decision Problem: "I really want that job badly. I haven't had a seizure for over a year, and the doctor says the drugs can keep it under control indefinitely. How can I answer that question and still get the job? Do you think I have to answer?" Ralph, a college senior, looks at you, the counselor, eye-to-eye, expecting an answer.

Ralph has come to you for help in finding a suitable job. He had dropped out of school three years ago and worked as an electronic equipment repairman before returning to campus to finish work toward a degree, and he is interested now in a similar job after graduation. He is well qualified and has a good chance of getting it except for one drawback—Ralph has a history of epilepsy.

You and Ralph know that employers often hesitate to hire people who have a history of epilepsy, and you both know that employment applications and interviews almost always include a question about emotional, physical, or mental disturbances. Ralph is asking you for advice on how to handle his interview and how to fill out his application. He does not think of himself as an epileptic since he has not had a seizure in a year. He feels it would not be dishonest to evade the issue. He is wondering what to do, and he wants you to give him advice on how to present himself in the best possible way.

Your Decision: As the counselor, how do you proceed?

STOP! Make your decision before proceeding.

Questions and Issues:
1. If Ralph asks you what you would do if you were he, what should you say?
2. Should you help train Ralph to present himself in the best possible terms during employment interviews?
3. Should you talk to the employer about Ralph? To his doctor? To vocational rehabilitation agencies?
4. Would you consider it unethical to imply in any way that Ralph might conceal his medical condition?
5. How long must a symptom be dormant before one is justified in saying he no longer has a particular condition? Symptom could refer to epilepsy, anxiety, depression, drug habit, homosexual act, and so forth.

Further Involvement: Try to determine if employers do discriminate against epileptics, diabetics, amputees, former mental patients. Such discrimination may be very subtle, and a questionnaire item to employers, "Do you discriminate (yes   ) or (no   )," may not get the real answer.

**What
Actually
Happened:**

The counselor had encountered several instances of employer prejudice against hiring "emotionally disturbed" people. Therefore he agreed to help Ralph present his history in a positive way. He told Ralph not to state on the application blank that he had epilepsy, even if directly asked. The counselor wanted to be sure that Ralph would be granted an interview where he could personally state his case. They role-played employment interviews so Ralph could feel comfortable saying things like, "I did have epilepsy, but I don't any more. I haven't had an attack for a year."

A CALL FOR HELP

**Decision
Problem:**

One Sunday evening about 11:00 the phone rings in the apartment of a counseling psychologist who is interning at a university counseling center. The young man answers the phone and finds himself talking with one of his clients at the center, a twenty-year-old co-ed who has recently been released from a psychiatric ward after her fourth admission for suicidal attempts and depression. Since her release, she has been seeing the intern every week.

She is attractive and intelligent and the intern has had some difficulty dealing with her because he finds himself sexually attracted to her. She usually arrives late for the weekly sessions and does little talking, but recently she has been calling him at home and talking on and on. Tonight as the intern listens to her, she threatens to commit suicide unless he comes to her apartment. He wonders what to do. Should he refuse to see her and risk the chance of suicide? Should he see her and perhaps strengthen her tendency to threaten suicide to get her own way? Or is there some compromise he can accomplish?

**Making the
Decision:**

Before you decide what the intern should do, carefully consider each of four alternatives.

1. See the girl immediately. If the intern sees the girl, he may be reinforcing her attempts to manipulate him. He is also placing himself in a precarious position. Regardless of where he sees her—his home, his office, or her home—he will be in a position to be accused by the girl of making sexual advances should she care to do so.

2. Refuse to see the girl. Since there is no foolproof way of assessing suicide potential, the therapist is assuming a great

deal of responsibility. If the girl feels rejected or merely angry, she may actually attempt suicide and may accidentally injure or even kill herself.

3. Refuse to see the girl but explain your feelings about her and explain the compromising aspects of a visit at that hour to her apartment. This approach may make the girl feel better, but it changes the nature of the therapeutic relationship and again places the counselor in a "one-down" position. The client is probably more likely to continue her manipulative efforts if she knows of the counselor's attraction to her. She may be likely to misperceive the nature of the counseling relationship and profit little from counseling.

4. Refuse to see the girl but provide other help for her immediately and later. In this case, the counselor would tell the client he would see her in his office in the morning, and if she felt incapable of controlling herself, she could check into the mental hospital or the student hospital for the night. He might also offer to check with her doctor about possible medication. If she were still unresponsive and continued to threaten suicide, he could tell her that he would ask police to take her to the hospital. Police are reluctant to intervene when someone is only threatening suicide, but the girl would probably be unaware of this. Although this alternative could be dangerous, if it worked it would foil the client's attempt to manipulate him while showing her that he is still concerned about her and is providing for her.

Your Decision: You are the intern holding the phone in your hand. What are you going to say to the girl?

STOP! Make your decision before proceeding.

Questions and Issues:
1. What do you do with suicide threats which may or may not be used to manipulate others?
2. How does one separate personal feelings from professional responsibilities to be able to recognize when the latter may be used as an excuse to act because of the former?

Further Involvement:
1. Role-play the 11:00 P.M. telephone conversation.
2. Find out what policies the counseling center and the psychiatric service at your school have about out-of-office-hours contacts.

What Actually Happened: The intern did go to the client's apartment because of the urgency in her voice and because he thought she was in danger of committing suicide. He spent about an hour calming her down and trying to reduce her depression until she had herself under control. The next morning he realized that nonprofessional feelings might have been involved in his decision to see her. He gave a sigh of relief that the incident was closed, and he made a mental note to choose another alternative if it happened again. With sunlight filling his office, he decided he had acted unwisely.

9

What Should Be Told to Others?

When a prospective student applies to a university, his entrance application becomes a matter of record and is kept in a permanent file by the school. The longer a student remains at an institution, the fatter his file becomes, filled with information of varying kinds. Some is personal data supplied by the student, and some is descriptive or evaluative data written by professors, high school teachers, deans, advisors, and, occasionally, by doctors, housefellows, ministers, and student personnel people.

The student may or may not want others in or out of the institution to have access to the information. Whether the student likes it or not, some people may need to study the folder in order to help him, while others also may be entitled to have access to it. What information is a parent entitled to have? The first case in this chapter deals with the question, What can or should be told to a student's mother over the telephone?

THE CONCERNED MOTHER

Decision Problem:
Bob, an assistant dean in a large university, wondered what he was going to tell Mrs. Johnson tomorrow. She had just called from New York to talk about her daughter, June, who had phoned home earlier that day to tell her parents she was withdrawing from school. Mrs. Johnson told Bob that since June was a senior, her grades were not sent home. She never wrote so they had no idea what was really going on. She then asked Bob to give her June's grades and to tell her how June was doing "mentally" and what kind of disturbing situation she was getting into.

Bob didn't know June's grades, and he didn't have any facts about her current plans. He said as much to Mrs. Johnson while trying to convey a concerned and helping attitude. Mrs. Johnson then asked him to call June into his office and talk her into staying in school. The mother told him she was concerned

80

about her daughter but did not want her to think she was interfering. She forced an agreement from Bob that he would not tell June she had called. "Anybody could see," she had said, "that the best decision for June to make was to stay in school." She wanted to know how the university could possibly let a student withdraw without telling the parents. She asked Bob to call her back the next day, and her parting words were, "June has been acting strangely lately, and somebody in the university should find out what is going on before something dreadful happens. Won't you please help her? I won't do anything until I hear from you tomorrow."

Making the Decision: Bob thought of several questions after he hung up the phone. What is June's status with the university? Is she emotionally upset? Can she be reached? If so, how can he contact her without revealing her mother's call? If June has withdrawn, doesn't she have the right to be left alone?

"If I'm going to call Mrs. Johnson back in the morning," he thought to himself, "I better get some answers fast." Pulling out June's folder, he discovered that she had withdrawn the day before. There was a note in the folder stating that she and her parents had been fighting for several years about her college plans. Her parents wanted her to finish, and June knew her mother would be furious when she found out about the withdrawal. June's plans were indefinite, but because of failing grades last semester and this, she would not be able to graduate at the end of the year anyway. There was also mention of a boyfriend and of possibly getting a job.

Bob checked her grades and saw that she was an art major with better than a *C* average. She could graduate if she made up three incompletes from last semester and satisfactorily completed the courses she was taking now.

Your Decision: If you were Bob, what would you do? Call June? If so, what would you say to her first? What questions would you ask? What items of information would you give Mrs. Johnson when you called her back?

STOP! Make your decision before proceeding.

Questions and Issues:
1. Do you think it is ethical for Bob to call June without mentioning that her mother had called?
2. What information should be provided routinely to parents about their college-age children?

3. Should the following information be provided if parents specifically request it?—(a) their child's major; (b) evaluation of their degree progress, such as grade-point average, number of credits completed, and whether they are on probation; (c) their plans, vocational decisions; (d) interpretations of test scores, any other information or opinions about probability of success; (e) statements in folder about what the student has said concerning college life, his friends, values, and so on.

4. How does one verify, during a telephone conversation, the true identity of the caller? How should telephone requests for information he handled?

Further Involvement:

1. Obtain a confidentiality of information policy statement from the appropriate source at your university. Comment on its adequacy and make suggestions that you think would improve it.

2. Discuss the ethics involved in trying to talk somebody into staying in school even "for their own good."

What Actually Happened:

Bob called June and asked her to come in early the next morning to discuss her withdrawal. He told her he thought there might be some problems that he could help her with, and that he could at least clarify her reasons and discuss future plans with her. He did not mention that her mother had called.

June answered by saying there was really nothing to talk about. She had withdrawn from school, would be working, and did not intend to return to school in the near future. She said she would come in later to see him if she felt she needed help.

She talked coherently over the phone and could discuss her affairs in a calm, reasonable manner, so Bob decided to investigate no further. The next morning he called Mrs. Johnson, told her June had withdrawn from school, and as far as he could tell, she knew what she was doing and was not emotionally upset. He said the university could not intervene in June's life, and if Mrs. Johnson wanted more information about her daughter, she would have to talk directly to her. He gave her June's address and telephone number which were listed in the student directory.

DO PROSPECTIVE EMPLOYERS HAVE THE RIGHT TO KNOW?

Employers want personal histories of prospective employees, and they often request information from universities. The typical graduate has a "clean" record, and it is a routine duty for any dean of student affairs or registrar to provide a transcript, verify that a particular person did, in fact, receive a degree, and even state that there is no evidence of emotional illness.

Colleges are willing to do this if the student requests it. What should a university do when it receives a request from a person who claims to be a prospective employer but no request is received from the student? This is one of the issues in this case. A second issue is concerned with providing information when there is an unresolved question about a student's character or morality. Keep these two problems in mind as you put yourself in the place of the dean of students at Southwestern University.

Decision Problem: Mr. Benson, dean of students at Southwestern University, is impatiently waiting for his last appointment of the day. An FBI agent wants to talk to him about Harry. Last fall, after consulting with the academic dean, a local police detective, and a legal advisor in the president's office, the dean had reluctantly decided to let Harry stay in school. The evidence was not sufficient, Mr. Benson was told then, to obtain a conviction in court, and there appeared to be no academic basis for suspension.

Earlier in the fall a fire had been discovered in a tool shed adjacent to a dormitory cafeteria. A night watchman had put out the fire before much damage was done. From material found in the shed, a detective established that the fire had been deliberately started. Police had questioned Harry after his sister had confided to a friend (who told police) that she was convinced Harry had set the fire. The police found another student who had seen Harry at a bus stop one block from the dormitory about 1.00 A.M., an hour after the fire was thought to have been started.

Harry denied setting the fire, claiming he had been in a bar. The bartender remembered seeing him but thought he had left before the bar closed at midnight. Harry refused to take a lie detector test. Further investigation revealed that police in Harry's home town had suspected him of setting fire to an abandoned automobile but had been unable to get sufficient evidence to arrest him.

Also during the investigation, the detective talked with several of Harry's friends. One of them was an admissions counselor for the university and had known of the fire as well as the sister's suspicions concerning Harry's involvement. He had said nothing of it to anyone until he was questioned by the detective. The detective had told Mr. Benson he thought the counselor friend should have voluntarily said something earlier and that perhaps he knew more than he was telling even now.

At the time of the investigation, Mr. Benson had thought of talking with the friend who, as an admissions counselor, was under his jurisdiction, but he had decided against it. Nor had he ever talked with the director of admissions about the case. He did ask police to watch Harry and his counselor friend, which they did for the rest of the year, but there were no further fires on campus and no new evidence. Harry graduated in June.

Your Decision:

You are Mr. Benson and your secretary brings your visitor into your office. He introduces himself as a member of the FBI, shows his credentials, and says that Harry has applied for a government job in Washington and has tentatively been promised the job contingent on a security check. This is necessary because the job involves handling classified information. In checking with local police, he was told that you knew Harry. That's why he is here to talk to you. What are you going to tell him?

Your Second Decision:

You are still Mr. Benson. Later the same summer, the admissions director casually mentions to you that one of his good counselors is leaving and is applying for a job as assistant admissions director at Southwestern State. You discover that it is Harry's friend, and you ask yourself if you should say anything to anybody about him. If you don't, no one else will, because no one else who would be asked for recommendations knows about the Harry affair. It had been kept very quiet. Are you going to say anything about Harry's friend?

STOP! Make your decisions before proceeding.

Questions and Issues:

1. Do you think the dean should tell the FBI man about the arson charge against Harry?
2. Do you think the dean should tell the admissions director about Harry's friend?
3. When should information about a student be given to a prospective employer when the student has not requested it?
4. What policy differences should there be regulating the release of information to wife, parents, prospective employer, draft board, graduate school, loan office of local bank, police, advisor, department chairman of student's chosen major, a professor?
5. What do you do when a student requests that all available information be released to a prospective employer but you

have information that is detrimental to the student that he doesn't know you have?

Further Involvement:

1. After considering the questions and issues, draft a policy statement that sets guidelines for the release of information by staff members of the university.
2. You are a registrar and you receive the following letter. How will you react?

Dear Sir:

    Please send my transcript to the Johnson Company. I have applied for a job with them.

                                    Sincerely,

                                    John Jones

Enclosed with the letter is a note from John Jones asking you to forward his letter to the Johnson Company with a note from you stating that the university will not send the transcript.

What Actually Happened:

    The dean of students told the FBI man that Harry had been accused of arson but that the charge had not been proven.
    The dean did not discuss Harry's friend with anyone. He was not asked for a recommendation, and he did not volunteer any information.

THE ANXIOUS TEST TAKER—PART I

In the Harry case, an outside source requested information but no direct request was received from the student. In this case, a student requests that information be sent to an outside source that has not asked for it and, in fact, may not want it. This raises a new question, How much should one inquire about the attitude of the person who is being given information?

Foreword:

    You are almost through your first year as a counselor in the counseling center of a medium-sized western university.

Decision Problem:

At 8:00 P.M. on the last day of final examinations, you receive a phone call from Henry H. He apologizes for bothering you at this hour but says the situation is urgent.

He tells you he flunked his history exam, did poorly in other tests, and is going to be dropped from the university. He says that he studied for his history exam and knew the material well, but just before the exam he became so anxious his mind went blank.

He talks on, telling you that after the exams were graded, he contacted the history teaching assistant and explained to him all about his test anxiety problem, how it had bothered him for a long time, and that he was getting help at the counseling center. He claims that the T.A. seemed very understanding and told him he could take a different kind of exam and count it instead of the first one if his anxiety problem were verified by a professional counselor.

Henry pleads with you to call the T.A. immediately to verify his history of test anxiety. Grades have to be turned in tomorrow, and unless the T.A. hears from you tonight, he will turn in the *F*.

Making the Decision:

Henry had voluntarily started coming to see you about six weeks ago. Before every important test he became so nervous, he couldn't sleep, couldn't concentrate, developed an upset stomach and diarrhea. He wanted to stay in college and was functioning well in other areas of his life. He did well in courses requiring papers instead of exams, but examination grades were ruining his academic record and affecting him emotionally. You feel that Henry is making some progress with counseling.

Your Decision:

Are you going to call the T.A.? If you call him, what are you going to say?

STOP! Make your decision before proceeding.

Questions and Issues:

1. Is it ever appropriate for a counselor to provide information or a professional opinion to a third party at the request of a counselee? If your answer is yes, when?
2. Write a general policy statement dealing with this issue that might be followed in a university counseling center.

Further Involvement:

1. Check with several offices in your school that handle student records and find out what confidentiality policies they have. Are policies the same in all offices?

2. Role-play the telephone conversation between Henry and the counselor.

What Actually Happened:

The counselor called the T.A. and said it was possible that Henry really knew a great deal more than his history test score might indicate, and he explained Henry's anxiety problem. The counselor said he knew grades were a matter for the instructor, but Henry had asked him to give this information to the T.A. It was a short conversation. The T.A. thanked him for the information and hung up.

THE ANXIOUS TEST TAKER—PART II

Decision Problem:

The week after finals, the counseling center director called in the counselor and told him that he had received a complaint from a professor about ethical behavior. Professor Turner in history had called to report that the counselor had attempted to persuade a T.A. to change a grade that was fairly given in accordance with departmental procedures.

The director asked the counselor to tell him about Henry. The counselor thought a moment and responded, "Well, I've been working with him for seven or eight weeks. He has a history of freezing up on exams even when he knows the material. Objective and multiple-choice exams are especially bad for him; essays don't bother him as much. College is important to him, and I thought we had been making progress.

"But then he really bombed his history final and went in to talk to the T.A. afterward. According to Henry, the T.A. was sympathetic and said if he could verify the existence of a test anxiety problem, he would be glad to record an incomplete instead of an *F* and give him an essay test. So, I simply called the T.A. to verify the anxiety problem."

Next the director called the T.A. to get his side of the story. The T.A. said he was confused. The student had flunked several history exams and had to get an *A* or *B* on the final, which was an essay exam, or flunk the course. Henry nagged him to regrade the exam and give him another chance. He threatened and pleaded until the T.A. was "fed up." Just to get rid of him he said he would listen to the counselor if he called.

When the counselor called and suggested Henry knew more than his test score indicated, the T.A. decided he didn't know what he was talking about, thanked him, and turned in the *F*. Later, while having coffee with Professor Turner, the

T.A. casually mentioned Henry and the counselor's call. He hadn't meant to get the counselor in trouble and had only mentioned it to the professor by chance.

Finally, the director called the registrar's office and learned that Henry had not flunked out even with the *F*. The director reviewed these details with the counselor who decided he had made a mistake in calling the T.A. He should have checked facts first, and he should not have acted so hastily or been so gullible. The director thought a valuable learning experience had occurred, and he said nothing more to the counselor.

Your Decision: If you were the counseling center director, would you now call Professor Turner and/or the T.A.? If your answer is yes, what will you say?

A POTPOURRI OF REQUESTS

Custodians of university student records receive hundreds of requests each year for information. Most of the requests are routine, such as a student asking that his transcript be sent to a prospective employer, but there are a surprising number of requests that are not routine. Some requests, asking for information that is readily available as public information, can be filled without violating any confidence and without student agreement. The university's problem with these requests is clerical; it takes a great deal of time, money, and personnel to process each request.

Other requests for information come from special interest groups or businesses seeking student names for mailing lists. Here are ten requests similar to those received by universities all over the country.

Decision Problems:

1. A local life insurance company asks for the names and addresses of all graduating seniors so it can send them literature explaining the advantages and variations of life insurance.

2. The Student Committee to End the War in Vietnam asks for names and addresses of all veterans so it can send them literature explaining the Committee's purposes.

3. A local Catholic church requests the names and addresses of all freshman Catholics so it can contact them.

4. The Student Association requests names and home addresses of all students listed by city so student senators can keep their constituents informed over the summer months.

5. Mrs. John Sams phones to say that she has moved to 100 Drury Lane to stay with her sister while her husband goes to summer camp. She requests that his final grades be sent there instead of to the address on file.

6. The Office of Teacher Certification in a neighboring state asks for a student's transcript. The request claims the student has applied for a teaching license in that state, and that to process the application, they must have an official transcript. The transcript must be received within ten days or the student will not receive his license in time to teach that fall.

7. The student health director asks for information about a student's grades, academic standing, progress toward a degree. The student is not under treatment at the health center, but his father is assistant director of the center. A note in the student's folder speaks of parental intervention and negative student reaction toward father's intervention.

8. The state vocational rehabilitation agency wants all available information about a student so they can determine whether he is progressing satisfactorily. They want assurance that the information comes directly from the university and that the student has not had a chance to change any of it. Unless they get the information, the agency says it cannot continue financial support and payment of the student's tuition.

9. A professor asks for information about a student because he is concerned about the student's poor performance in his class and would like to see what the student's test scores indicate about his academic performance or scholastic ability.

10. A father asks for grades of his twenty-two-year-old daughter who is a senior. He claims a psychiatrist who is treating his daughter requested the grades.

Your Decisions: You are the registrar of the university and your office contains the cumulative records of all these students. How will you answer each request?

1.   6.

2.   7.

3.   8.

4.   9.

5.   10.

10

Professional Programs

Professional programs, such as law, business, pharmacy, education, and others, create their own set of problems because they have assumed the obligation to protect their collective reputation and society from incompetent and unscrupulous practitioners. Potential students in these programs are screened, and those who do not meet the standards are cut. The screening process can take place before admission, during or at the conclusion of the program.

There are wide differences of opinion about when the screening process should take place and about what criteria to use. The four cases in this chapter represent different aspects of the special problems confronting professional programs. The first case tells about a student who has been admitted into a professional program, but because of subsequent behavior, his professional attitude is questioned.

SCOTCH IN THE ROOM

Decision Problem: You, Coach Williams, are looking over basketball plays when the dean of student affairs calls to report that Dan, a senior physical education student, has been placed on social probation and that a reprimand has been put on his record because he was caught with a bottle of Scotch in his room which is contrary to dormitory regulations.

You are thinking that having a bottle of Scotch in a dorm room isn't such a major crime when the dean continues to explain that a dorm housefellow accidentally discovered the Scotch while investigating a commotion caused by a girl running down the hall screaming, "He's after me!" The girl had run out of Dan's room. The door was open. The housefellow spotted Dan's roommate, nude, smoking marijuana. A search of the room turned up the Scotch but no more marijuana. The dean also tells you about an incident the year before when Dan had gone to a neighboring town, had a few beers, gotten into a fight, and had been thrown into jail.

You thank the dean for the information and chew your gum much more violently than you did before the phone rang. You know Dan has just applied for a student teaching assignment which must be approved by the department, and you are the representative assigned to approve or disapprove such requests. If you approve Dan's application, you would, in effect, be saying you know of no negative evidence concerning the character of the applicant.

Your Decision: How are you going to handle Dan's case?

STOP! Make your decision before proceeding.

Questions and Issues:

1. Once the coach decides to let Dan continue, what obligation does he have to observe Dan's behavior? What obligation does he have to mention the Scotch and jail incidents on any recommendations he writes for Dan? Remember, these incidents are facts, even though Dan may not realize they will affect his reputation as a potential teacher.
2. In this case, Dan was already in the program when the coach had to decide whether or not to cut him. Suppose the dean of student affairs had called with the same information before Dan had been admitted into the program. If you were the coach and your recommendation would admit him, would you agree to his admittance request?
3. Should professional programs cut students who have bad habits, negative attitudes, character defects, antisocial tendencies, and so on? How should the screening be done? What criteria should be used? Should a student who has been cut have the right to appeal?

Further Involvement:

1. Try to determine what procedures are used in a professional school of your choice to screen students. Are these procedures well defined or are they vague? Suggest changes you think would be appropriate.
2. After you have decided whether or not to approve Dan's student teaching application, consider these two slightly different versions.

   If Dan had a record of several drinking arrests, including one for assault, would your decision be different? yes_____ no_____.

If Dan had been caught smoking "pot," would your decision be different? yes____ no____. If he had been caught selling "pot"? yes____ no____.

What Actually Happened: The coach decided to question Dan about his attitude toward teaching before he considered his student teaching application. He called Dan into his office and told him he knew about the Scotch and jail incidents. He warned him that such behavior caused the department to question his suitability for teaching, and that he was seriously considering not approving Dan's student teaching application.

Dan appeared surprised and genuinely concerned. He said he wanted to be a physical education teacher, and he thought he would make a good teacher. He said he never thought that "horsing around" in college had anything to do with his fitness to teach. Now that he knew his behavior outside the classroom was important, he wanted a chance to prove he could stay out of trouble.

The coach checked with other faculty who knew Dan. All of them thought he had good potential as a physical education teacher. He finally called Dan back into his office and told him he would approve his application, but that if even one negative incident were reported to him, Dan could expect unfavorable recommendations at the end of the year.

THE PERPETUAL STUDENT

Most applicants for admission to professional programs come directly from undergraduate programs, but some do appear after they have been in the service or have worked, or have transferred from other programs. Occasionally such an applicant has a truly unique career development pattern which creates interesting problems.

Decision Problem: The admissions director of the school of education at a major university had just finished interviewing Mr. Jimson, an applicant for the teacher-certification program. According to Mr. Jimson's transcripts, he graduated with honors in premed and entered medical school, but he had voluntarily withdrawn when his father died. He told the director he was an only child, and he felt his mother needed him at home.

While living at home, he completed a second undergraduate degree in English with excellent grades and then began work on a master's degree in a biological science. He dropped out of that program and took a job. About three years later his records indicate he was admitted into law school, went one semester and transferred into speech. He had also been in the Army for three years. During the interview, the director learned that Mr. Jimson is now forty-four years old and working as an assistant in the public library.

The admissions director thought of Mr. Jimson as a pleasant, unassuming, cultured, and well-educated man. He tended to ramble in his conversation but was knowledgeable about community affairs, world affairs, recent books, history, and philosophy. He told the director he had finally decided to become either an English or a speech teacher. He had brought with him a note from a speech professor asking that he be given a chance.

Several days after the interview the director asked a natural science professor who had known Mr. Jimson ten years earlier about his potential. The professor told him that Mr. Jimson was intelligent and could easily get A's and B's, but that he had never amounted to anything, was indecisive, and couldn't manage his own affairs. He was completely dependent on his mother for advice, and in the professor's opinion would be unable to maintain classroom discipline.

Mr. Jimson would be back to see the director for his admission decision. The director knew that if admission were denied, he would want to know why.

Making the Decision: Academically Mr. Jimson qualifies; however the criteria for admission also state that an applicant must have "suitable character for teaching." On the basis of his record, the director could refuse to admit Mr. Jimson to the certification program. He could also admit him, admit him on probation, or try to persuade Mr. Jimson to voluntarily cancel his application.

Your Decision: As director, what are you going to tell Mr Jimson?

STOP! Make your decision before proceeding.

Questions and Issues:
1. Some graduate departments will not admit applicants over forty. Should age be an admission factor?
2. Should unusual career patterns be admission factors?
3. Should professional evaluations about immaturity, lack of judgment, instability, inability to manage a classroom situation be admission factors?

Further Involvement:

1. Survey one or more graduate departments to determine to what extent they would answer "yes" to questions 1, 2, and 3.
2. Debate the question, "Does every person have a democratic right to enter a profession?"

What Actually Happened:

If two applicants apply for a teaching position, Mr. Jimson and a recent graduate, a superintendent is undoubtedly going to choose the latter. There is a definite prejudice against hiring older people who are applying for their first teaching job. Should older teacher applicants be told this? In this case, factors other than age are significant. Although Mr. Jimson is very intelligent, he has never succeeded in a profession, and he has constantly changed the type of career he wants. The best prediction is that he will never realize stable employment as a high school teacher.

The director reached this conclusion and decided to have a talk with Mr. Jimson again. He carefully detailed the negative factors in the case. Mr. Jimson insisted that he could make the grade and that he was more qualified by virtue of his experience than were younger teachers who lacked his understanding of natural science, philosophy, and related matters. He was admitted to the certification program, but because of his inability to relate to adolescents, he was dropped from the program.

THE STUDENT WHO LIKED LITTLE BOYS

Decision Problem:

Mr. Carlton, a member of the educational psychology faculty at the university, and Sister Theresa, a teacher in a local parochial school, were chatting during an education conference. Sister Theresa suddenly asked, "Do you happen to know a graduate student in counseling by the name of Jack Jahr?"

Mr. Carlton said that he did, indeed, know Jack Jahr. Before he could say more, Sister continued, "We have been delighted with him. He voluntarily started a youth choir at our school and he does wonders with those little boys' voices. I didn't know he was a graduate student until he told several of us last week that he would finish course requirements for a master's degree this spring and will be looking for a job as a school counselor next fall. We can't afford to hire a replacement for him, so I'm afraid the choir will fall apart. He's a charming young man and probably won't have any trouble finding a job."

When the conference ended, Mr. Carlton walked back to his office, wondering what obligation he had to do something about a chance remark during a casual conversation. He had met Jack Jahr two years ago when Jack had come to see him about beginning work on a master's degree in counseling. During that interview, Jack had told him about two unpleasant incidents in his past.

While teaching in a small-town high school, he had started a choir of fifth, sixth, and seventh graders at his church, and after several months, someone started the rumor that he was "up to something" with the little boys. There was no trial, but Jack's teaching contract was not renewed, and he was asked to leave the community.

He found a nonteaching job in another town and once again started a church youth choir. Rumors began again. This time he was arrested and convicted on a child molesting charge but was placed on probation under psychiatric supervision.

At the time of the interview, three years had elapsed since the second incident, and no further trouble had occurred. Jack had married, and Mr. Carlton remembered that he seemed well adjusted, but he had not encouraged him to go into counseling. Jack had a personnel-type job then, and Mr. Carlton had suggested he might take a few graduate courses for his own personal advancement.

Mr. Carlton had not seen Jack since the interview, and he had almost forgotten about him until today's conversation with Sister Theresa.

Making the Decision: If you were Mr. Carlton, would you say anything to Sister Theresa? If so, what? Although Mr. Carlton did not have Jack in any of his classes, does he have an obligation to the department to reveal what he knows about Jack to prevent him from getting a master's degree in counseling?

STOP! Make your decision before proceeding.

Questions and Issues:

1. Do you feel that Jack should have been admitted to any graduate program? To a graduate personnel program in particular?
2. If you cannot give a clear-cut yes or no to either of these, what additional information would you want? How would you suggest obtaining that information?
3. If you were Mr. Carlton and a prospective employer asked you for a recommendation for Jack, would you feel obligated to mention the dismissal and conviction?

Further Involvement:
1. What personality factors should bar an applicant from school teaching, counseling, or administration? Examples might be chronic alcoholism, homosexuality, rape, narcotics addiction.
2. What antisocial behavior should bar an applicant from a similar job? Examples might be battery against a police officer, child beating, desertion from the armed forces. (It should be noted that each of these examples has been taken from actual cases.)

What Actually Happened:
Mr. Carlton did not say anything to Sister Theresa. He checked with Jack's advisor and was told that Jack was not contemplating returning to public school work. Mr. Carlton made a note to himself to check on Jack's activities in a few months. He told himself he would have to say something to Jack or to his advisor if Jack were to return to public school employment.

THE BEARD

At one time, students in professional programs tended to be conservative in dress, appearance, and often in ideology. This case is an example of how entrenched professional interests are discovering that the professional aspirants of the early 1970s do not fit the stereotype.

Decision Problem:
Shortly before 8:00 one Monday morning, Peter arrived at a suburban high school to begin his student teaching assignment. When he reported to his supervising classroom teacher, she told him that the principal liked to talk with student teachers on their first day in his school, so he went immediately to the office and introduced himself. The principal opened the conversation by telling him he would have to shave off his beard if he wished to stay in that school. The principal added that he had no hard feelings, but Peter was not to return if he kept the beard.

The principal's action came as a complete surprise to Peter. He had already met the supervising teacher, and she had not questioned his beard, at least not to him personally. Replying to the principal's ultimatum, Peter said he felt he had a right to wear a beard and cited eminent people in history who wore beards. He said the beard did not affect his teaching ability, and he believed it was part of the learning process in a democracy to stand up for individual beliefs. He wanted to teach his students not to give in to an arbitrary, capricious rule for which there was no reasonable argument of support.

Peter informed the university director of student teaching of his problem and asked what should be done. The director thought of Peter as a well-mannered, well-dressed young man whose character and grades were excellent. He had worn a beard for about six months and kept it well trimmed. The director knew Peter wanted to teach history in a high school and needed student teaching for his degree and certification. The director called the principal to discuss the situation with him personally but was told the decision was final. Next he called another high school in the same district and asked that principal to take Peter. The principal was sympathetic but said it would complicate his relationship with the other school if he took Peter after he had been rejected by the first school.

Finally, the director called the superintendent of schools who said he personally had nothing against beards, but a superintendent had to back up his principals and that's what he would have to do in this case.

**Your
Decision:**   If you were the director, what would you do now?

STOP! Make your decision before proceeding.

**Questions
and Issues:**
1. Do you think student teachers should be required to conform to the dress standards of the school in which they student teach?
2. If the university secures a student teaching assignment for a student, does its obligation to the student end if he could meet school requirements and expectations but will not do so?

**Further
Involvement:**
1. Role-play a dialogue between the principal who won't give in and the student who will not cut off his beard.
2. Obtain a copy of a dress code for a local school system, both student and faculty, and discuss its "fairness." Interview students and teachers in the system for their reaction to the code.

**What
Actually
Happened:**
The school's reaction caught the director of student teaching off guard. The principal explained that he believed allowing a beard in the school was the first step toward disorganization and flouting of other school rules. He had a rule that none

of his regular teachers could wear a beard, and it would be unfair to allow a student teacher to wear one.

The director had placed another bearded student in a neighboring town, and although some of the older teachers had been rather distant, things seemed to be going smoothly. Remembering this, he decided to contact schools in other districts, and on his third try he found a school that would accept Peter, beard and all. He did a good job and received excellent recommendations.

11

Faculty Tyrants

Faculty autonomy is a precious acquisition, and professors guard it jealously. At some universities its power is akin to that of salaries in luring new teachers, and just as a professor may use his salary wisely or unwisely, so may he use his autonomy wisely or unwisely. Proper use of faculty autonomy can result in an unfettered and diligent search for knowledge by students as well as teachers.

Improper use of faculty autonomy can create a restrictive atmosphere for other higher education participants that is incompatible with the educational purpose of a university. Taking untempered advantage of the situation, a professor can subject his students to irrational outbursts about his personal opinions and prejudices and can unjustly penalize them when he evaluates class work and awards final grades. In short, faculty autonomy can create a faculty tyrant!

Awarding grades is a difficult assignment for the most conscientious professor. What is a "fair" grade? What is the difference between a C grade and a D grade? Can a professor prove his grades are fair, or can a student prove the opposite? Because of the great importance attached to the grade point system and the uncertainty of the grade-giving process, students complain. Most students do not attempt to have a grade changed, largely because they think it is impossible to do.

There is the occasional student, however, for whom a particular grade makes a great difference and who trys to do something about the "unfair" situation by talking with a relevant authority. That authority then has a difficult decision to make. What, if anything, should he do? Some student complaints simply are not valid, but there are legitimate reasons for many others. The people involved are not always sure who should handle the complaint or how each case should be treated. These three cases deal with circumstances where an older person has almost autonomous power over students, and at least one student in each situation has gone to a relevant authority to complain.

99

OPINIONATED ART PROFESSOR

Foreword: You are an art professor serving as advisor to juniors in the art program. One of your advisees is Julie whom you consider to be mature and responsible in her approach to college work. You have not had her in a class, but you have discussed her plans with her several times.

Decision Problem: Julie bursts into your office carrying a large canvas and, fighting back tears, tells you she's just received her second *D* in an art course from Professor Amsley.

"He hates me," her voice becomes defiant, "and he does everything he can to discredit my work. One of the paintings I did for a class assignment even won second prize in a local art show. Here, you look at this," and she turns the canvas over and holds it up for you to see.

According to Julie, Professor Amsley does not consider her work to be true art, and he constantly degrades her and her art publicly. She tells you she defended herself in class once and made him appear ridiculous before the other students, and since then he has never given her a fair break. "I get good grades in every other art course," she says.

Julie desperately wants to continue her art career. She is being considered for an art scholarship and for admission into a graduate art program, and she is worried that two *D*'s will ruin her chances for acceptance.

When Julie finishes her story, you glance at her transcript which she has handed you and notice that in art classes she has six *A*'s, four *B*'s, and the two *D*'s from Professor Amsley. You lean back in your chair and quickly think of Professor Amsley. It's his first year on campus, and you don't know much about him except that he has a national reputation as an artist and that a couple of other students have complained to you about his sarcastic, opinionated manner.

Julie interrupts your thoughts, "What can I do about this? Isn't there somebody who can protect students from harassment by unfair teachers?"

Your Decision: As her faculty advisor, what are you going to do or say?

Further Decision: Suppose you are the chairman of the art department and Julie comes to you with the same story. What will you do?

STOP! Make your decision before proceeding.

**Questions
and Issues:**

1. What should an advisor do when students challenge the legality or fairness of a professor's action? Should he intervene or champion their cause in any way?
2. Whose role is it to intervene when students make accusations about the appropriateness of a professor's evaluation of their class work?
3. Would an ombudsman be of help in Julie's situation? How might he proceed?
4. How is it possible to determine whether an art professor's evaluation is valid or fair?

**Further
Involvement:**

1. Role-play Julie's dialogue with her advisor.
2. Ask faculty members what recourse they feel a student should have from a professor's grade.

**What
Actually
Happened:**

Julie's advisor listened sympathetically. He discussed details of her work in art classes with her and said he could understand why she was upset but that he was in no position to determine whether or not Professor Amsley's grades were fair. He suggested she contact the chairman of the art department. Julie became even more agitated when he said he could not help her, and she left his office as abruptly as she had entered.

DELAYED PLANE INCIDENT

Foreword:

When students miss examinations, it is customary to excuse them for a death in the family or for illness. Are these the only reasons for which excuses should be granted? Who should be the judge when a professor challenges the validity of a student's excuse? In this sequence, place yourself in Gail's seat as you return for your freshman midterm examinations.

**Decision
Problem:**

Gail fastened her seat belt and stared out the window as the big jet nosed straight up from the runway. She was only casually aware of the receding ground as her mind focused on the night ahead. Her plane would be in Chicago by 8:00 P.M. She would have just an hour to catch a second flight to Midwestern University, arriving at 9:30 P.M. She could study for her exams for three hours and still get to bed by 1:30 A.M.

Her first exam was the next morning at 9:00 with a second one at 1:00 P.M. This schedule would leave a couple extra hours for review between tests. Gail leaned back in her seat and tried to relax.

She had spent an exhilarating weekend in the East, visiting friends, skiing, and looking over two college campuses. She wanted to transfer to one of them, but she was too tired to think of that. She would rest on the plane and think later. The impending exams didn't worry her. She had studied before the trip, and she was doing well in most of her classes except for that sociology course, the exam at 1:00 P.M.

She had not hit it off well with the instructor. Gail thought of herself as a serious student, but he had typed her as a playgirl, all because of a late paper incident. Several times he had thrown sarcastic remarks her way, so now she was afraid to speak up in class. She reminded herself she had studied hard for this exam, and with a decent night's sleep plus a last-minute review in the morning, she could really show him that she was a serious student. She desperately wanted good grades in these courses so she would be able to transfer.

Gail jerked as the pilot's voice announced through the loudspeaker that the plane would be delayed briefly. The jet landed at an intermediate stop and Gail's schedule was smashed as an hour and a half slipped by. Finally the flight was routed around Chicago and into Milwaukee at 3:00 A.M. Gail arrived at her dorm at 6:30 A.M., too keyed up to sleep. She ate breakfast, reviewed her notes, showered, and went to her first exam. She couldn't concentrate, and she knew she wasn't doing well, but her biggest concern was her 1:00 exam. As soon as she finished, she went to her sociology professor to explain the situation and to ask if she could take his exam later. She was almost relieved when he wasn't in his office.

She left a note explaining that an emergency had come up and that she would get in touch with him later that afternoon. She returned to his office about 3:00 P.M. and tried to explain that she had missed the test because her plane was late and she had not slept at all. She was very nervous and contradicted her own story. When the professor told her she would not have planned a weekend trip just before exams if she were really a serious student, she made some unnecessary remarks. He rejected her excuse, she cried, hating him for making her cry, and left in an emotional state bordering panic. She hurried back to the dorm, anxiously discussed the situation with her roommate who calmed her down and finally got her to sleep.

While Gail was eating breakfast the following morning, she asked herself, "What do I do now?"

Your Decision: You are Gail. You've gotten yourself into a jam. What will you do next?

STOP! Make your decision before proceeding.

Questions and Issues:	1. What circumstances serve as valid excuses for missing classes, handing in papers late, making up tests?
	2. How can these excuses be substantiated? For example, is a student's statement that he was sick sufficient proof?
	3. What can students do to minimize personality clashes with professors?
Further Involvement:	1. Show your list of valid excuses to several professors and students and see if the two groups agree with your list. Ask them the substantiation question (No. 2 in Questions and Issues).
	2. Role-play Gail's confrontation with the professor.

What Actually Happened: Gail was upset with herself for losing self-control in the professor's office and for confusing her story. She was also upset with the professor because of his misjudgment of her character and his lack of understanding. Partly because she felt sorry for herself and partly because she thought she might get some support, she went to see the assistant dean in charge of student affairs of her college. She told him her story and asked if there were any way he could help her straighten things out with the professor.

Another Decision: If you were the assistant dean, what would you do?

STOP! Make your decision before proceeding.

What Actually Happened: The dean wondered to himself whether the reported incidents in class and the account of the plane trip were literally true or were exaggerated in order to make her case more plausible. He then wondered whether the plane incident was really an excuse comparable to an illness or a death in the family. If so, he would be justified in contacting the professor. They discussed various possibilities and concluded that since she would have to continue dealing with this professor, she should make an appointment to see him, making sure there was privacy and time to talk (not just after class) to discuss the whole semester with him, especially asking him what she could do for the future so that she could still get a good grade.

Gail told the dean she would come back to tell him how she and the professor got along during their talk. However, she didn't come back, and the assistant dean had the feeling she really wanted him to explain the plane incident to the professor, giving it the validity of a legitimate excuse. He wondered if he should have done that.

THE AGING DORMITORY HEAD RESIDENT

Recent discussions have gained much substance from the generation gap, the differences in values and morals between those who are older and those who are younger. When those who are older have some authority over those who are younger, the latter sometimes have their plans overruled. An example of this situation is found in the following case.

Foreword: Assume you are director of dormitories, chief administrator for the entire dormitory system, in a large midwestern university. Each of the ten dormitories in the system is managed by a head resident who lives in that dormitory and who is responsible for its operation.

Decision Problem: You listen intently as the student president from one of the dormitories tells you that the head resident will not approve plans for a dorm party. The president explains that it is not the first time this year dormitory student officials and housefellows have been thwarted in attempts to have fun and do something different.

"The head resident wants everything to stay just like it's always been," the president says. "She doesn't approve of new ideas, and she's always making disparaging remarks about the younger generation. She just won't listen to us at all."

You ask the student president several questions and promise to look into the situation further. The student leaves and you begin to review the case in your mind.

This is not the first time that you have had a complaint about this particular head resident. She's within two years of retirement and has spent her entire professional life in service to the university. Lately she seems to have become set and rigid in her ways. You know she doesn't listen to the students, and since she has alienated most of the people with whom she has contact, she's no longer effective in her work. You sigh. The girls' plans sound like fun and seem reasonable. Should you overrule the resident and OK the party? What would this do to her and to the whole administrative structure of the dorms? Finally you resolve to talk the situation over with her.

You arrange a meeting that same afternoon, and as you talk, it becomes apparent she will not back down on the party issue. Furthermore, she's irritated because the girls bypassed her and went to you. Her parting words are "As long as I'm head resident, there'll be no parties like that." What are you going to do?

Making the   Before making your decision, consider the advantages
Decision: and disadvantages of each of the following alternatives.

1. Allow the students to have their party and in a separate conference tell the head resident what you have done. (Remember, you thought the party plans were reasonable.)
2. Tell the head resident she should approve this party or you will overrule her.
3. Support the head resident's decision but warn her she will have to come to some understanding with the girls and in the future approve plans that are comparable with what other dorms are doing.
4. Do nothing (she will retire in two years).
5. Support the head resident's decision but try to work out a different arrangement within the dormitory for future approval of social plans.

Your   Which of the foregoing decisions would you make?
Decision:

STOP! Make your decision before proceeding.

Questions   1. What is the role of a director or any employer when students
and Issues: under the jurisdiction of a subordinate complain about treatment by the subordinate?
2. What qualities should the executive head of a dormitory possess? How can one determine when such qualities are present?
3. How should an executive head be appointed? For how long should the appointment be?
4. Who should have to live in dormitories? Who should have first preference?
5. Discuss with others the advantages and disadvantages of each of the alternatives mentioned earlier.

Further   1. Role-play a scene in which the director tells the head resi-
Involvement: dent he is transferring her.
2. Design an ideal governing system for a dormitory. Indicate how students are to participate. Indicate job responsibilities for each person in the system.

What   The director supported the head resident in this decision.
Actually   He talked again with the girls, letting them know he was giving
Happened: careful consideration to the situation. He said he saw nothing wrong with the party, but the decision within each dormitory

was the concern of the staff and residents, and he would not want to interfere with that decision.

Next he talked with others in the dormitory complex and ultimately concluded that the head resident's continued presence in that dormitory was detrimental to healthy dormitory life. He discussed his conclusion with her and arranged a transfer to another branch of student affairs where she would work with application processing and eligibility determination. She would be able to work in that office until retirement.

Part Three

Decision Processes and Situational Responses

12

Decision-Making

Criticism of individuals in higher education is often criticism of the decisions these people make. Critics are saying, "So and so made a bad decision. It should have been done this way instead." Usually campus decision-makers are experienced and competent. If one should have made a different decision, why didn't he? Is it possible that he thought he had made a good decision? Can a decision be both good and bad? When are criticisms of decision-makers really justified? How does one make good decisions?

The business of making good decisions is the subject of this chapter. By carefully examining the concept of "good decision," it becomes apparent that "good" is largely an illusion—a product of people rather than of decisions. Examine an eating decision. Pork, steak, and shrimp are edible foods. A decision to eat one of them is good or bad, right or wrong, depending on the person making the decision. Is he a Catholic? A Jew? A Hindu? Is he allergic to seafood?

Since the goodness of a decision is an evaluation made by people and since people differ radically in their values, it is clear that almost any position can be taken toward any decision. It is clearly impossible for a decision-maker to protect himself from all critics. He can, however, reduce the risks of criticism by understanding various decision processes and by becoming competent in the process of making decisions. Much of this chapter is directed toward achieving these purposes.

EVALUATING DECISIONS

No decision is good or bad in and of itself. How it is evaluated by people gives it its value. This observation is true of a wide range of decisions—going to college, buying a house, vacationing in the wilds of Alaska, eating horsemeat, cutting out a tumor, becoming a carpenter, buying uranium stock.

"Good–bad" judgments depend on a number of situational conditions and individual values. A first fact about decisions is to recognize that any label, good or bad, right or wrong, is a projection of the one who attaches the label and may have little to do with the actual decision. When a person talks about the goodness of a decision, he is saying much more about his own values and perceptions than he is about the decision. When persons disagree about the goodness of a decision, they are talking primarily about differences in their own personal values. These differences refer to specific things and events, the usefulness of various decision processes, the responsibility of man, and criteria by which a decision should be evaluated. The first of these, differences regarding specific things such as bananas, plane rides, class absence, is widely recognized, and little need be said about them. Differences regarding more complicated aspects of decision-making are worthy of further exploration, for they often are not completely understood. They account for the use of a variety of decision processes and for much of the prevailing criticism of decision-makers.

DECISION PROCESSES

It is useful to distinguish between decision process and the product of that process, the actual decision. Process refers to the decision-maker's thoughts and actions which relate to and culminate in the actual decision.

Process varies from person to person and can include gathering information by reading, exploring, consulting; interpreting dreams; reading the stars; reciting nursery rhymes such as Eeny, meeny, miny, mo. . . .; dissecting dog livers; and an interesting variety of other methods (see Cohen, 1964). A process can be a continuous, an intermittent, or a single act, or it can be a complex sequence of events. It can be overt or covert.

Because people have different beliefs and values, they employ different decision processes. Mary Smith consults an astrology chart, but Jane Doe wants to know what her friends think. John Jones scoffs at both and says he wants facts, while Tom Tinker says it's the principle that counts and decides on that basis. Mary, Jane, John, and Tom each believes his particular kind of process is best, and each might be critical of the process used by the others.

In a given instance, there is no real way of knowing whether a person's explanation of his process accurately describes how his decision was made. He may not be aware of all the ingredients of the process he used or he may deliberately present his process in a distorted way. This could be the case if he wanted to be thought of as a "good" decision-maker by a person advocating another process. Such problems make it difficult to study decision processes used by good decision-makers.

Seven Decision-Making Types

People employ simple and complex processes. Simple processes can be grouped into seven basic types. Each can result in a decision, but whether that decision is good or bad depends on the person evaluating the decision. The complexity results by incorporating all or parts of two or more simple processes into complicated chains. The seven basic types are (1) follow an accepted rule, (2) utilize a rational process, (3) act to gain social approval, (4) follow your intuition, (5) leave it to fate, (6) arrange a compromise, (7) consult an expert.

Using the "follow an accepted rule" process, a decision-maker arrives at the appropriate decision by applying what he considers to be a relevant rule to the decision situation. A university has a rule that an applicant must be in the top half of his graduating class. An application arrives stating that the applicant is in the bottom half of his class. The admissions director writes him that he is not admissible. A little girl is stopped on the street by a man in a car who wants to take her for a ride. She remembers her mama's words, "Don't ever get in a car with strangers." She replies, "No thank you," and runs around the corner.

Rule, in this case, covers any written or verbal statement or thought of such statement that provides the decision-maker with a sufficient basis for action in the situation. Such statements stem from a variety of sources: law, philosophy, parental edicts, moral or ethical codes, superstitions, science, and religion. A decision-maker can apply the first rule he thinks of, or he can refer to several and apply the one he feels is most appropriate or most powerful. Rules can be combined into sequences and can include "if" statements as part of a sequence. If it is raining and you don't want to get wet, carry an umbrella. If it is raining and you don't want to get wet and you don't have an umbrella, wear a raincoat. One could add a provision for staying inside during periods of high winds or lightning. Experienced bridge players make use of complicated sequences of rules. Computers can be programmed with a number of sequences so they can play chess or shoot rockets to the moon.

Making a decision by rule is a very common method of deciding. The method works well in situations that repeat themselves regularly. The method is quite efficient in terms of manpower, time, money, energy, and maintaining emotional stability. But in novel or ambiguous circumstances where conflicting rules can be applied or in changing societies when accepted rules are being vigorously challenged, the rule-applying process has its limitations.

The second method, "utilize a rational process," refers to decisions that are made as a result of considering the expected consequences. There are several versions of this process. Using one variation, the decision-maker first considers the alternatives and then considers the outcomes of these alterna-

tives. He estimates the probability of occurrence for each outcome and indi-
cates what numerical value he places on each outcome. He multiplies the
value by the probability. For each alternative he adds the products for those
outcomes associated with a given alternative, giving him a number represent-
ing the expected value for each alternative. He then maximizes, that is he
chooses the alternative with the highest number.

To illustrate the process, we use a condensed version of a going-home-
from-work decision taken from Bross (1965). The stated alternatives are
drive a car or take a bus. Bross lists outcomes of the first alternative as "arrive
home early and without incident, arrive home late due to traffic delays or
accident." Outcomes for the second alternative are "arrive home early and
without incident, arrive home late due to missed connections." At this point
the decision process looks like this:

ALTERNATIVES	OUTCOMES
1. Drive a car	a. Arrive home early and without incident
	b. Arrive home late due to traffic
	c. Accident
2. Take a bus	a. Arrive home early and without incident
	b. Arrive home late due to missed connections

Bross estimates the probability of (1a) as .85, (1b) as .145, (1c) as
.005; (2a) as .1, and (2b) as .9. Bross views value in terms of cost and
assigns cost values to the outcomes as follows: (1a) = $.0, (1b) = $1.00,
(1c) = $50.00, (2a) = $.0, and (2b) = $1.00. Bross indicates costs as
negative values.

The calculation for the expected value of the drive-a-car alternative is
$(.85 \times .00) + (.145 \times -1.00) + (.005 \times -50.00) =$ expected value.

The calculation for the expected value of the take-bus alternative is
$(.1 \times .00) + (.9 \times -1.00) =$ expected value.

The alternative with the highest expected value is the "best" decision
using this method.

Brim, et al. (1962) outlines a method where value is indicated in terms
of scale values instead of dollar costs. Brim feels value can be indicated as
$+2$ = strongly desire, $+1$ = desire, 0= don't care either way, -1 = do
not desire, -2 = strongly do not desire. The reader might substitute what
he feels to be appropriate desirability scale values for the cited cost values in
the Bross car example and rework the calculations. Numbers, of course, will
vary from decision-maker to decision-maker because of differences in values.

The rational process is not new, but it is both lesser known and more
complicated than the using a rule process. Edwards (1967) has traced it

back at least as far as Bernouli. It has been widely used in the economic world and has been considered the best single decision process (Edwards, 1965). Other versions are discussed in Bross (1962) relative to the going-home-from-work decision presented here.

The rational process provides techniques for and stresses the quantifying of probability and value. In practice such numbers are elusive or unreliable, and a shrewd guess may have to suffice. Numbers and techniques for combining them help make a more exact decision, but the key concept in the rational process is not number or technique; it is attempting to anticipate probable consequences of various alternatives for action and then to choose in consideration of these probable consequences.

Using the "act to gain social approval" process, the decision-maker knows or finds out what relevant people value and then decides in consideration of these values. Relevant is defined by the decision-maker. One aspect of such a process is aptly illustrated by the phrase, "keeping up with the Joneses." If my neighbors have new cars, I have to buy one too.

When stated as "keeping up with the Joneses," the process seems to have a negative connotation. The decision-maker's behavior is controlled largely by others. But when used in other ways, the process has a more positive meaning—a car manufacturer decides to survey a sample of people to get opinions about the styling of a new car before he actually markets it; or a politician lets prevailing opinion in his precinct decide a matter for him.

How useful is the social approval method? One needs friends, family, employer, and the support of the community. In many situations, making decisions to gain their support makes a lot of sense. There are times, however, when their support is neither necessary nor needed. If one always acts to please others, he becomes a sycophant and is not generally regarded as a person with character, leadership ability, or responsibility. Other processes are necessary to maintain personal identity and to decide issues of no social import or issues where social forces have conflicting values.

People who use the "follow your intuition" process make decisions almost without thinking. One song phrases it as "doing what comes naturally." The decision is impulsive, reactive, in consideration of the moment. Merchants know that if they display items attractively and intimate they are bargains, shoppers will buy them impulsively.

The question must be asked, Are impulses or intuitive actions really decisions? We treat them as decisions because some people do accomplish intuitively what would require a more thoughtful decision process by others. The irresponsible, carefree, and the existential approaches to life stress intuitive and spontaneous decisions. There are many mature, responsible people who can trust their intuition, but there are others who are always in trouble because of some crazy impulse. Most people can and do respond intuitively in many daily decision situations. The question is, Is this a good way to resolve major decisions of the type normally faced by participants in higher education?

The "leave it to fate" decision process includes a variety of methods. Most are viewed in western civilization as amusing, irrelevant, or illogical. Such methods include palm reading, consulting mediums, reading astrology charts, and interpreting dreams. Any process for solving problems that involves chance, luck, or accident belongs in this category. So do all processes involving an outside source which has no known or logical relationship with the real world. Fate and lady luck are common expressions for such a source.

When a decision must be made but there is no real basis for a decision and the decision-maker wants to remain neutral, fate processes are as useful a way of deciding as man has yet been able to devise. An example would be flipping a coin to determine the winner in an election where two candidates tied. Whenever possible, however, man feels that human thought can do a better job than fate.

Following the "consult an expert" process, a decision-maker lets another person recommend a decision for him. Presumably, the other person has more information, better understanding, and more experience with whatever must be decided and therefore is capable of making a better decision than the decision-maker. Consulting a lawyer about legal matters, an architect about house design, an accountant about financial matters are common examples. If a "phony" expert, who lacks real knowledge or who advises because of an ulterior motive, is consulted, the process may fail to produce useful results. The advantages of experts are recognized, but a person seeking one should be capable of sorting out pretenders. In the case of troublesome decisions in higher education, there are not many experts available who have had much experience.

"Arrange a compromise" process is self-explanatory. Bargaining with a merchant over the price of an article for sale and management bargaining with a union to reach a wage settlement are common examples. A compromise agreement is a joint decision that is beneficial to at least two parties, but perhaps not as beneficial as either had originally wanted. If one party will not compromise, a different process must be used.

There are similarities among the different processes. For instance, some rules can be stated in social approval terms, "Son, shake hands when you are introduced to an adult." A desirability value can be put on social approval and that value may be attached to particular outcomes and incorporated in the rational process. Or, one can have a rule to consult an expert or a rule to compromise. Compromise can be viewed as striving for maximum social approval, and so the similarities continue. However, differences remain if only in the thinking of the decision-makers. Recognition of these differences is implied by adjectives used to describe people: compromising, conforming, law abiding, deliberating, impulsive.

In a stable society, the majority of people have common values and consequences are predictable. A great many decisions are easily made by knowledgeable individuals—intuitively, rationally, following an accepted rule or in consideration of social approval. The decision tends to turn out as expected, and no questions about processes are asked.

In a rapidly changing society where groups of people are challenging other groups, where the young will not adopt traditional values, and where consequences of changing conditions are not easily predictable, even knowledgeable individuals using any or all processes are going to have decisions go sour. Then the process is questioned. It may be that regardless of the process or the product, some decisions will be rejected by some group. Literally, the decision-maker can't win.

APPLYING THE PROCESSES

Let us reexamine the Perilous Job Interview decision in chapter 3 as a "can't win" type of decision and see which of the seven decision-making processes would be most helpful. In this case, a university president was confronted by a group of students demanding that Company X be barred from coming on campus to recruit employees. The students said that if necessary, they would physically prevent the company's recruiting because it manufactured war material.

An intuitive decision by the president could go either way, depending on how he responded to the immediacy of the situation. He could reach into his pocket for a coin to flip if he decided to let fate make the decision for him. He could consult experts to advise him, but in this situation it is not obvious who the experts are, whether they might agree or disagree among themselves. The president, then, could use any of these three processes to help him with his decision.

If the president tried to apply the rule process, he would have discovered that at the time of the confrontation there were no specific rules pertaining to conditions under which interviews should be cancelled, how students could be prevented from interfering with interviewees' right to interview, how to act in the face of threatened disruption, possible student-initiated violence, or how to control student mobs on campus and in buildings. The president's authority is designated in very general terms and does not automatically indicate what he can, or even should, do in specific situations like this. Because there have not been similar situations on his campus, he does not have a precedent to follow. What might an accepted rule be?

Following the social approval process, the president would seek out relevant groups to determine how they feel about the situation. He calls faculty members from all disciplines and asks what they recommend. Some tell him the interviews should be held and police called in if necessary. Others are outraged at the idea of bringing police onto a college campus, pointing out that this has never been done before and would create a dangerous precedent. Another group says that the right to dissent must be protected, and yet another wants to find a compromise position and prevent student versus student violence at all costs. The president cannot determine the number favoring each solution. The alumni association tells him to follow a strict line, but the student association directs him to follow a soft line. The president sadly concludes he cannot gain social approval from all parties by following any one course of action.

If he tries the compromise process, he will probably not succeed either. The dissident students claim they can't speak for the hundreds of students who favor disrupting the interviews. Many faculty and alumni are not in favor of compromise because that would be "giving in" to the students.

Using the rational process, the president thinks of alternatives: (1) hold the interviews as scheduled, (2) hold the interviews but change time and/or place, (3) cancel the interviews, (4) talk Company X into cancelling or changing the interviews. He tries to calculate the probabilities of the consequences that might occur from each, but ends up guessing, because in this situation there is really no way of calculating a probability. Are the students bluffing? In this case any of the processes could result in a decision, but would it be a "good" decision? In cases like this, does it make any difference which process is used?

DEFENSIBLE PROCESSES

Seven decision processes have been examined and applied to a troublesome decision. In any decision situation, all or none of the processes may achieve similar results depending on chance, acts of God, amount of information available to the decision-maker, and the values of the decision-maker, plus the value of those who will evaluate it. Except for the "leave it to fate" process, all processes incorporate personal values so that different people using the identical process can make different decisions. As has been stated, whether or not a particular result is good depends on who is asked to evaluate the decision. Some evaluators would judge on the basis of how it was made, others on what happened afterwards, and some on what was actually decided.

Does this mean that it makes no difference how one makes decisions? Does this mean there is no point in trying to make good decisions since the decision-maker can't be sure of the outcome? Not at all! He may not win a particular decision situation, and he may never win according to a certain percentage of people, but he can come out ahead over a long period of time and with a majority of evaluators. How? By competently following a defensible decision-making process.

Think of the Job Interview case again and compare a decision-maker who considers alternatives, consequences, and how people might evaluate his decision and then decides to hold the interviews as scheduled, with a decision-maker who decides to hold the interviews as scheduled after flipping a coin. Society formulates ideas of what man should do. When he does what is expected, he is viewed as acting reasonably. His actions are defensible; people are less critical and more supportive. In the Job Interview case, people would say it is better to exert best judgment than to abdicate personal responsibility and let "Lady Luck" make the decision.

In situations where consequences of actions are not easily predictable, it is unreasonable to expect man to accurately predict them. However, it is reasonable to expect him to try to anticipate possible consequences and to make an effort to determine which ones are more likely to occur. It is unreasonable to expect man to know in advance exactly how groups of people will react to events that have never occurred before, but it is reasonable to ask him to try to assess what the reaction might be. If he has tried to gather as much information as possible, consulted with relevant others, thought out the possible effects of various alternatives, he has done three things. He will be more likely to achieve desired results than if he had done nothing. He has followed a process that a reasonable person would be expected to follow in order to make an important decision, and he has followed it competently. Is it reasonable to expect more?

What does *competently* mean? Decision processes are not automatic. Each contains the possibility for foolish actions, and the decision-maker is expected to obtain the maximum potential of the process. He is expected to maximize influencing factors so that they work to his advantage. In betting on a dice game, the competent decision-maker is on the lookout for loaded dice. In consulting an expert, the competent decision-maker will try to determine whether the expert has ulterior motives. In determining social approval, the competent decision-maker will try to obtain an unbiased sample.

What does defensible process mean? It is simply the series of actions that people expect other people to follow in particular kinds of situations. There is a great deal of ambiguity in that statement, and readers can find examples of decisions where people differ as to what actions are expected. But that's the way the world is, and there appears to be no immediate change in sight, especially in our changing society with the crucial decisions facing participants in higher education. The best one can do is shrug off uninformed criticism, be less critical of others caught in similar situations, and competently try to follow a reasonable decision process as consistently as possible.

13

Reply, If You Can!

The assistant dean sat at his desk, listening intently, his mind trying to grasp the dynamics. Georgia sat in a chair to the right of his desk, nervously fingering a book in her lap. Her parents sat across the desk from the dean, talking rapidly, interrupting each other.

They said they were thinking of taking Georgia out of school because she wasn't doing very well, and they saw no reason for keeping her on campus if she wasn't getting anything out of the college experience. The mother assured him they had Georgia's best interests in mind and wanted to do the right things for her. Georgia wasn't mature enough to make her own decisions, she added. The father started to say that wasn't quite how they felt, but the mother gave him a quick glance, and he murmured some irrelevancy instead.

The dean took advantage of the slight pause to ask Georgia how she felt about leaving school. She replied that she was getting something out of school and was enjoying campus life. Before her mother interrupted again, she also said she was old enough to run her own life without interference, and she would prefer making her own decisions.

The assistant dean sensed there were many hidden issues and remnants of old arguments that were influencing the discussion. He also sensed that Georgia saw herself as the underdog in this fight and that the parents were looking to him as an objective authority to support their position. Almost in unison the three people asked him what he thought about Georgia staying in school.

As the assistant dean, what will you reply?

Previous chapters have contained decisions in logical units of related subject matter. You, the reader, were informed about what was coming, and you were given a chance to put on a good performance. Unfortunately for participants, troublesome situations do not always come wrapped up in neat little packages. Decisions are troublesome, in part, because of the abruptness of their arrival. Confrontations often occur when one is not prepared.

Here are fifteen "quickie" confrontations which involve the unexpected and the awkward-to-answer question. In each case, frame an answer, then compare and evaluate the answers suggested by other class members. Role-playing each confrontation adds to the effectiveness of the answers.

You are a student personnel worker or administrator in a setting appropriate to each of the following. You are required to respond to the other person in the situation.

1. Student, asked by professor to show cause why an *F* should not be recorded for a missed exam: "I missed the test because I attended my grandfather's funeral last week. I suppose you want a written note from my mother, just like when I was in high school."

    You:

2. Influential alumnus: "Look at this article in the campus underground paper. It calls the president a two-faced tool of military interests, uses four-letter words to describe the administration, and advocates that marijuana smoking be made legal. Are you going to let them continue writing this kind of stuff?"

    You:

3. Student: "Are you a trained psychologist? I don't think you'll be able to help me. I have some serious problems."

    You (a master's in student personnel or counseling):

4. Honor student: "What does an *A, B,* or any grade really mean? I've tried to get a satisfactory answer but continue to draw a blank. How can you defend a system that has no real meaning?"

    You:

5. Visiting legislator: "Why can't you people do something about the kooks you've got? This Joe Potts, whom I've been reading about, is always dirty and unshaven and uses filthy language publicly! He was arrested three weeks ago on a marijuana charge and he's still around. And there are more like him!"

    You:

6. Freshman: "I was always a good student in high school. Now I come here and can't really get going. What's wrong?"

You:

7. Depending on what the situation is at your university, respond to *a* or *b*:
   a. "Why should parents be sent a copy of our grades? We should be treated as adults not children."
   b. "Why shouldn't parents be sent copies of student grades? After all, we pay the bills and our children are legally minors."

You:

8. In the following situation, the first two statements made by the local businessman are supported by facts and you know it. You also know that the university has taken a stand against further reductions in quotas of out-of-state students admitted.

Businessman: "Isn't it true that a higher percentage of out-of-state than in-state students are involved in the picketing and disruption maneuvers on this campus?"

You:

Businessman: "Isn't it true that recent disruptions have interfered with other students' rights to attend regularly scheduled lectures?"

You:

Businessman: "Why then don't you support the bill in the legislature that would reduce the number of out-of-state students on this campus?"

You:

9. Student: "Professor X gave me a *D* in first-semester calculus. I know there is some mistake, but he won't let me see my final exam paper. I talked to Professor X and then contacted the department chairman, but he referred me back to Professor X who told me the final grades have all been turned in and the case is closed. Then he told me to have a nice summer, all the time knowing I need a *C* in calculus to be eligible to take second-semester calculus next fall. I don't know what to do. Isn't there someone who can help me?"

You:

10. Freshman girl: "My older sister, Ann, dropped out of school and is dancing at that go-go place on the edge of town, but she hasn't told our parents yet. Our mother suspects something is wrong. She wrote me last week asking what Ann is doing, whether she is still in school, why she doesn't write, and why the phone in her apartment has been disconnected. I'm worried about Ann, too. She has changed lately and is running around with a different crowd. What should I do?"

You:

11. Local citizen: "I'm taking a class under Professor Newbeed. He tells students he doesn't care if they attend class or not and he knows there's a rule that says they should. He lets them smoke in class even though there is a 'No Smoking' sign right behind him. Disrespect for law and order is becoming a major problem. What kind of example does he set? How can a major university condone such practices on the part of its staff?"

You:

12. Sophomore: "I understand I need a 2.2 grade-point average to enter your Business School. I have a 2.1 right now. Can I be admitted? A career in business is what I've always wanted."

You (with authority to admit borderline cases but knowing that the faculty generally wants to maintain its standards):

Sophomore (if your answer was anything other than an unqualified yes): "Now suppose by the end of next semester I have raised it to a 2.15, could I be admitted then?"

You:

Sophomore (if your answer was anything other than an unqualified yes): "What about a 2.18, 2.19, or 2.195? Could I get in then?"

You:

13. Senior: "Why can't upperclassmen who have demonstrated their academic ability at this institution be allowed to take all of their electives on a no-grade (pass-fail) basis?"

You:

14. President of Student Association: "Professor Stodgy uses a textbook that is ten years old, and he talks about issues that are not relevant for today's society. The class is completely worthless; ask any of the students who have had it. Why is such a class required? Why do we have to take it under him? Why is he allowed to continue this exercise in required irrelevant monotony?"

You:

15. Police Detective: "We picked up Miss Mary Moore in a drugstore trying to obtain a dangerous drug by using a forged prescription. She said the prescription was another girl's and that she was just picking it up for her. I would like to have a sample of her handwriting so we can match it against the handwriting on the prescription. Will you give me a paper with her signature on it?"

You (with a folder that contains several of her signatures on routine business forms—like registration materials):

Bibliography

BRIM, O. G.; GLASS, D. C.; LAVIN, D. E.; and GOODMAN, NORMAN. *Personality and Decision Processes.* Stanford, Calif.: Stanford University Press, 1962.

BROSS, IRWIN, D. *Design for Decision.* New York: The Free Press, 1965.

CARDOZIER, V. R. "Student Power in Medieval Universities." *Personnel and Guidance Journal,* vol. 46, no. 10 (1968), pp. 944–949.

COHEN, JOHN. *Behavior in Uncertainty,* London: George Allen, 1964.

COX COMMISSION REPORT. *Crisis at Columbia.* New York: Random House, Inc., Vintage Books, 1968.

EDWARDS, WARD; LINDMAN, HAROLD; and PHILLIPS, LAWRENCE D. "Emerging Technologies For Making Decisions." *New Directions in Psychology II.* New York: Holt, Rinehart and Winston, 1965, pp. 261–325.

EDWARDS, W., and TVERSKY, AMOS. *Decision Making.* Baltimore, Md.: Penquin Books, Inc., 1967.

FLACKS, RICHARD. "Student Activists: Result, not Revolt." *Psychology Today,* vol. 1, no. 6 (1967), pp. 18–24.

GELATT, H. B. "Decision-Making: A Conceptual Frame of Reference For Counseling." *Journal of Counseling Psychology,* vol. 9, no. 3 (1962), pp. 240–245.

HALL, MARY H. "A Conversation with Kenneth Keniston." *Psychology Today,* vol. 2, no. 6 (1968), pp. 16–23.

HEINZERLING, LYNN. "What Are Student Agitators Trying to Prove?" Associated Press article reprinted in *Wisconsin State Journal,* April 13, 1969.

KERPELMAN, L. C. "Student Political Activism and Ideology: Comparative Characteristics of Activists and Nonactivists." *Journal of Counseling Psychology,* vol. 16, no. 1 (1969), pp. 8–13.

MUSCATINE, C. (chairman, Select Committee on Education). *Education at Berkeley,* Berkeley, Calif.: University of California Printing Dept., 1966.

RUBINSTEIN, ELI A. "Paradoxes of Student Protests." *American Psychologist,* vol. 24, no. 2 (1969), pp. 133–141.

WATTS, W. A.; LYNCH, S.; and WHITTAKER, D. "Alienation and Activism in Today's College-Age Youth: Socialization Patterns and Current Family Relationships." *Journal of Counseling Psychology,* vol. 16, no. 1 (1969), pp. 1–7.